# PRAISE FOR *ACCE[* *LEADERSHIP DEVE*

'A must-read for HR leaders who are charged with building a strong pipeline of leadership talent. Provides practical and effective solutions for accelerating leadership development all brought to life by powerful case studies and quotes from HR and business leaders.' **Maria Kokkinou, Vice President, Talent Management, Development & Inclusion, Coca-Cola European Partners**

'This timely book provides a compelling step-by-step guide, full of practical tips and examples from some of the world's most notable companies. An informative read for anyone involved in leadership development.' **Carolyn Fairbairn, Director-General, CBI**

'Good leadership takes courage and so does good leadership development. A well-written and extensively researched book that shows how HR must take bold people decisions to develop the next generation of leaders. Highlights the importance of diversity and inclusion throughout, and rightly so.' **Baroness Mary Goudie**

'Dr Wichert has written an excellent step-by-step guide on how companies should be thinking about, and executing, long-term development plans for their top talent. It is well laid out and easy to read: full of good examples of best practice and pitfalls to avoid. Essential reading for senior management, HR practitioners, as well as young leaders thinking about their own career trajectories.' **Dr George Olcott, Guest Professor, Faculty of Business and Commerce, Keio University, Japan**

'It is no longer about picking winners in the old school sense, but how we nurture outliers and make them succeed. This book could not have come at a better time where we need less promises and more strategy on the topic of diversity (age, gender, ethnicity). Companies may say they are committed to change and Ines provides a specific strategy on how to implement change and what that actually means for both the organization and the individual.' **Pauline Wray, Managing Director, Asia Head, Expand Research and Global Head of the Fintech Control Tower, a company of the Boston Consulting Group**

# Accelerated Leadership Development

How to turn your top talent into leaders

Ines Wichert

KoganPage

First published in Great Britain and the United States in 2018 by Kogan Page Limited

| | | |
|---|---|---|
| 2nd Floor, 45 Gee Street | c/o Martin P Hill Consulting | 4737/23 Ansari Road |
| London EC1V 3RS | 122 W 27th St, 10th Floor | Daryaganj |
| United Kingdom | New York, NY 10001 | New Delhi 110002 |
| www.koganpage.com | USA | India |

© Ines Wichert, 2018

The right of Ines Wichert to be identified as the author of this work has been asserted by her in accordance with the Copyright, Designs and Patents Act 1988.

ISBN    978 0 7494 8305 0
E-ISBN  978 0 7494 8306 7

**British Library Cataloguing-in-Publication Data**

A CIP record for this book is available from the British Library.

**Library of Congress Cataloging-in-Publication Data**

Names: Wichert, Ines C., author.
Title: Accelerated leadership development : how to turn your top talent into
   leaders / Ines Wichert.
Description: London ; New York : Kogan Page, 2018. | Includes bibliographical
   references.
Identifiers: LCCN 2018015019 (print) | LCCN 2018017773 (ebook) | ISBN
   9780749483067 (ebook) | ISBN 9780749483050 (pbk.)
Subjects: LCSH: Leadership. | Executive ability. | Employees–Coaching of.
Classification: LCC HD57.7 (ebook) | LCC HD57.7 .W5195 2018 (print) | DDC
   658.4/092–dc23

Typeset by Integra Software Services, Pondicherry
Print production managed by Jellyfish
Printed and bound by CPI Group (UK) Ltd, Croydon, CR0 4YY

*To Rosemarie*

# CONTENTS

# ABOUT THE AUTHOR

**Ines Wichert** is an occupational psychologist and has been working in HR consulting for over 15 years advising global organizations on their talent issues. She has a particular interest in leadership development and is the Founder and Managing Director of TalUpp, a leadership development consultancy that uses mobile technology and face-to-face solutions to help organizations develop the next generation of leaders.

Previously, she ran the Diversity & Inclusion Centre of Excellence for IBM's Smarter Workforce in Europe where she worked with global organizations on talent and leadership development solutions for diverse talent. Her last book *Where Have All the Senior Women Gone? 9 Critical Job Assignments for Women Leaders* was published by Palgrave Macmillan in 2011.

Ines has appeared on BBC News and has written and been interviewed for, amongst others, the *Financial Times*, *Wall Street Journal Europe*, the *Sunday Times* and various leading HR publications in the UK and abroad. She regularly speaks at events on the topic of talent management and leadership development.

She has a PhD in Organizational Psychology from the University of Cambridge.

# LIST OF INTERVIEWEES

Alexandra Aubart, Director Organizational Development, LSG Lufthansa Service Holding AG

Robert Baker, Senior Partner, Mercer

Dr Fiona Bartels-Ellis OBE, Global Head of Equality, Diversity & Inclusion, British Council

Brian Callaghan, Global Head of Leadership Development, Executive Resourcing & Corporate University, Global Steel & Mining Organization

Stephen Caulfield, Vice President Global Field Services & GM Dell Bratislava, Dell EMC Global Services

Sarah Chapman, CEO, Faro Energy

David Clarke, Global Head of People Capability, Syngenta International

Kristie Daloia, Manager, Mastercard

Andy Doyle, former CHRO, Worldpay Group plc

Jennifer Duvalier, Non-Executive Director, Mitie plc, Guardian Media Group plc, Royal College of Arts

Vera Gramkow, Global Head of Talent & Performance Development, Bayer AG

Rachel Gray, Sales Director, Experian plc

Michael Heil, Global Head of Talent Management, The Linde Group

Jo Hindle, Head of HR Asset Services, EMEA, Cushman & Wakefield

Laura Hinton, Chief People Officer, PwC LLP UK

Matthias Kempf, former Vice President Human Resources Emerging Markets, The adidas Group

Kim Lafferty, VP People Development, GlaxoSmithKline

Mary Lawrance, Founder, Cariance Executive Search & Consulting

Felizitas Lichtenberg, Global Diversity & Inclusion Manager, Vodafone Group

Uxio Malvido, Head of Talent Acquisition, Engagement & Inclusion, Lafarge Holcim

Dr Siobhan Martin, Executive Director UK HR, Mercer

Les Marshall, Head of Talent, NEX

Matthias Metzger, Global Head of Talent Management & Organizational Development, Continental AG

Selina Millstam, Vice President & Global Head of Talent Management, Ericsson

Raquel Montejo, Assistant Director, Learning & Development, IATA

Nicholas W Morgan, Client & Business Development Associate, International Wealth Management Firm

Alexander Nelson-Williams, Senior Management, Multinational Professional Services Firm in the 'Big Four'

Paul Nixon, Global Talent & Inclusion Relationship Manager (Europe, Australia & New Zealand), Mercer

Rachel Osikoya, Head of Diversity & Inclusion, Global Transportation & Logistics Organization*

Raquel Rubio Higueras, Global Leadership Development Director, IHG*

Sarah Sanderson, Head of Diversity & Inclusion Intelligence, Global Business Insight and Talent Consultancy

Torsten Schmeichel, former Global Head of People Development, Global Microelectronics Organization

Torsten Schneider, Director Human Resources, Luther Rechtsanwaltsgesellschaft

Dr Ursula Schütze-Kreilkamp, Head of Group HR Development & Group Executives, Deutsche Bahn AG

Catalina Schveninger, Global Head of Resourcing & Employer Brand, Vodafone

Michael Schwarz, Talent Consultant, Mercer

Ursula Schwarzenbart, Head of Talent Development & Diversity Management, Daimler AG

Susana Simões, Regional Lead EMEA, Learning & Development, Global Electronics Organization

Gillian Smith, Deputy Director, Head of Early Talent, Government Organization

Laura Tolen, Partnership Director, International Logistics Organization

Brendan Toomey, Vice President, Human Resources Asia Pacific, Hilton

Bella Vuillermoz, Director, Property Service Group, Sky UK

*\*Acting in a personal capacity*

*The views and opinions expressed in this book are the author's own and do not necessarily reflect the views of the interviewees or their affiliated organizations.*

# ACKNOWLEDGEMENTS

Many people have directly and indirectly contributed to this book and I owe them all my gratitude.

First, I would like to thank all the interviewees who made time in their busy lives to talk to me about their experiences of accelerated leadership development. Each engaged fully with my questions and shared their insights freely. Without their input this book would not have happened. It was a privilege to talk to each of them. Thank you.

I would also like to thank Lucy Carter and Stephen Dunnell at Kogan Page who helped bring this book to life. And I would like to thank Tamsin Martin, Simon Foster and Petra Edwards for their feedback on an earlier draft of this book. All three are leadership development experts and I have come to trust their knowledge and judgement in this area. Their comments were very helpful.

Finally, I would like to thank my family for their understanding and patience during the many weekends and evenings that the book took me away from them.

# Introduction

Many organizations have embraced accelerated development as the new norm. While some organizations already have well-established processes for accelerating their most promising talent in place and have given their topic a great deal of thought, others are only just embarking on the journey to make accelerated leadership development work for their organization. Most organizations are still trying to fine-tune their return on investment, as accelerated development can require additional resources. They are also still working on their return on risk, as accelerated development comes with additional risks for both organizations and individuals.

## The purpose of this book

I have worked in leadership development all my career, selecting and developing leaders at all organizational levels. I became particularly interested in the career development of women, who often suffer from stagnation rather than acceleration, and through my work as the Head of the D&I Centre of Excellence at IBM also started doing more work with organizations on their millennial populations, a group that many companies are keen to better understand and engage with more actively.

This book is inspired by the many conversations that I have had with colleagues and clients about the future of work and the need for a different breed of leaders. It is a continuation of the research I conducted for my last book, *Where Have All the Senior Women Gone? 9 Critical Job Assignments for Women Leaders*, where I explored the significance of 'stretch roles' for women's careers. This current book broadens this topic and adds to it the component of speed and the challenges of the VUCA (volatility, uncertainty, complexity and ambiguity) world. If we move promising talent through a set of highly developmental stretch roles at speed, and with the aim of developing them into leaders who can steer organizations through the rough seas of ambiguity, volatility and uncertainty, what do we need to put in place to make this happen successfully?

The book tries to address the fundamental questions of whether accelerating leaders is a good idea and if so, how organizations can do it safely and at scale. What are the building blocks of an acceleration strategy and what are the pitfalls to be aware of? What organizational culture do companies need to have in place and what individual mindsets do we need to foster to help create the right environment for acceleration?

While gender- and generation-neutral overall, the book briefly looks at the two talent groups that I have already mentioned: millennials who *want* accelerated leadership development and women who *need* accelerated leadership development. Zooming in on the careers of these two talent pools is not only a reflection of a personal interest of mine but also a good way to explore how any organizational strategy for accelerating talent must take into consideration the needs of different talent groups to be successful.

## How to use this book

The book aims to provide an in-depth exploration of the topic of accelerated leadership development, drawing both on original interview data as well as academic research. The interviewees, who gave up time in their busy lives to share their observations and insights into accelerated leadership development, can be heard throughout the book in the form of quotes from their interviews. Each chapter contains one or more 'In Practice' sections where the topic of the chapter is brought to life by personal or organizational examples. At the same time, each chapter contains a section of organizational design tips for HR practitioners as well as a corresponding section of coaching tips for individuals. The book is aimed at both HR practitioners and individual high-potential employees. As I will show in Chapter 2, accelerated development is always an interplay between an individual's desire for progression and their readiness to take personal risks with unfamiliar roles, and an organization's support of this personal ambition through formal and informal programmes and development solutions. As such, the book takes turns to explore individual and organizational aspects of acceleration and each chapter contains advice for both HR practitioners and individual high-potential employees. This set-up reflects a desire to show that both parties must work together closely to make accelerated development a success.

Each chapter is stand-alone and while it cross-references other chapters, it can be read in isolation, should the chapter's topic be of particular interest to you.

## The study

The book is based on two main sources of information. First, the book draws on in-depth interviews with 38 HR and business leaders and six millennial high-potentials, some of whom are already in leadership positions. Most of the interviewees work for large global organizations but the group also includes interviewees from SMEs, start-ups and public-sector organizations. The content and structure of the book were determined by the interview findings.

The second source of data, business and academic research, was used to further elaborate and explore the key themes that emerged from the interviews. Just under half of the HR and business leaders were UK-based (18/38) and the rest were based internationally (20/38) in countries such as Germany, Switzerland, Denmark, Sweden, Slovakia, Portugal, Dubai and Singapore. All millennial interviewees were UK-based.

# Tomorrow's leaders

01

## Succeeding in a volatile and uncertain world

*With AI, technical knowledge is no longer a differentiator. It is the individual that is now the differentiator. They need communication skills and to be able to communicate really complex issues in a meaningful manner. With data and analytics, how do we bring it to life for our customers? Our people need to build rapport and co-create. Technical skills are now only a base layer.*

LAURA HINTON, CHIEF PEOPLE OFFICER, PWC LLP UK

*Leadership is the key that opens the lock. Without good leadership we cannot achieve anything. Almost everything, including culture, new business areas, inspiring people or executing successfully on transformations, comes back to leadership.*

MATTHIAS METZGER, GLOBAL HEAD OF TALENT MANAGEMENT & ORGANIZATIONAL DEVELOPMENT, CONTINENTAL AG

## Organizations need good leaders

Organizations need good leaders. Leaders must continually transform their organizations to generate growth and stay competitive. This may mean growing operations in emerging markets, increasing an organization's size through a merger or acquisition, or divesting parts of the business that are no longer profitable. It can also mean building the most customer-responsive call centre or creating an industry-leading employer branding proposition that allows an organization to attract the best talent. Organizations need leaders at all levels of the organization and in all areas. When I talk about leadership in this book, I refer to leadership in its broadest sense: general managers, heads of department, functional experts and informal opinion shapers.

Leaders must inspire individuals to go beyond what is expected to generate exceptional levels of performance. Inspirational leaders develop powerful visions for their followers and create a culture of can-do, collaboration and innovation.[1] Furthermore, charismatic and inspirational leaders increase followers' levels of satisfaction by increasing feelings of empowerment and by creating cultures of trust.[2] Good leadership has been linked to increased individual, team and even organizational performance.[3]

Leading an organization, or any part of it, demands a broad range of leadership capabilities that allow a leader to deal with a host of challenges. However, good leaders are in short supply. Less than half of senior talent is recruited internally and attracting good external candidates is often cited as an organization's top challenge.[4, 5]

## In practice: the business case for accelerated leadership development

We are on a strong growth platform, so acceleration is important. We need to take exceptional leaders and then develop them well and quickly. If there is less of a growth platform then you can afford to take more time. M&A activity is an important factor for us, too. When we merged with another company of equal size, the EMEA CEO was leading a company twice the size of the original organization and the senior leadership's roles changed overnight. Outside of M&A activity, accelerated leadership development is still important as leaders will have to keep growing the business. And equally if there is a downturn in the market they must be best equipped to protect the business from being negatively exposed. This still requires strong leadership.

Jo Hindle, Head of HR Asset Services, EMEA,
Cushman & Wakefield

There are few organizations that are not in a state of transformation. Organizations need flexibility. And acceleration makes you more flexible and has a positive impact on execution. If we accelerate the path you are on, then you learn about accountability faster.

Jennifer Duvalier, Non-Executive Director, Mitie plc,
Guardian Media Group plc, Royal College of Arts

As the quotes in the In Practice box demonstrate, there is a clear business case for accelerating leadership development and many organizations already recognize the need for speeding up the development of their leaders. In a global survey of senior HR professionals at over 300 organizations, 85 per cent of respondents voiced their concerns about the current capabilities of their leaders and agreed that leadership development acceleration was a top priority.[6] In the same study, only 40 per cent of responding organizations stated that their high-potential talent can meet future business needs. Similarly, another study of senior HR and business leaders at global organizations found that 51 per cent of respondents regard their current leaders as incapable of leading their organization today, a number that rises to 71 per cent when respondents are asked to consider the capability of their leaders to lead the organization successfully into the future. Organizations feel that the profile of their current leadership population won't allow them to operate successfully in future business environments. This may not be surprising given the digital disruption that many organizations experience and the volatile and complex world they operate in.

The business case for accelerated leadership development is driven by two main factors – first, the *demand for more leadership talent*, which in turn is caused by the retirement of existing leaders, the need for more leaders in emerging countries and the career expectations of millennials. Second, the *changes in leadership capability*, which are driven by increased disruption and volatility in the business environment through phenomena such as digitalization and AI (artificial intelligence).

## Demographic changes and emerging markets

Capability shortages of existing leaders are further exacerbated by a lack of actual leaders. Every year, over 600,000 baby boomers are still retiring in the UK and every day, 10,000 are retiring in the USA. Most developed countries have an ageing population. Almost a quarter of the US workforce is over the age of 55.[7] Working-age populations will grow more slowly over the next 40 years and in some countries, such as Germany, Italy, France, Spain, Japan and Russia, they will start to decline. Globally, the share of older people, those aged 60 and over, is expected to more than double to about 21 per cent, or more than two billion people, in 2050.[8, 9]

Furthermore, the growth of emerging markets means that organizations must grow leaders who can operate in new markets. The world population share of current EU member states halved from 14.7 per cent in 1950 to 7.2 per cent in 2010 and is expected to drop close to 5.0 per cent in 2060. Equally, those of Japan, China and the US will be declining. In contrast, the world population shares of Africa, Asia and Latin America will be increasing. There will be one billion new consumers and three times as many large headquarters in emerging-market cities by 2060.[10, 11, 12]

## What millennials want

It is not only these external factors that demand a faster, more mindful development of leadership talent. The very people we want to keep in our organizations and nurture for future leadership roles are the people who want stretching roles and to move up the career ladder at pace. High-potential millennials are driven by career progression. They want meaningful leadership roles where they can have an impact.[13, 14, 15, 16] We will take a closer look at the career expectations of this future leadership pool and how organizations can keep them engaged and developing fast in Chapter 10.

It is therefore not surprising that acceleration of leadership development is an important topic for the majority of HR and business leaders who took part in the interviews for this book. For them the business case for acceleration is clear. Only a small number of interviewees stated that accelerated leadership development is not a key consideration for their organization due to a lack of staff turnover or flat organizational structures. There is clear pressure on organizations to grow the next generation of leaders. And it is not only a matter of replacing retiring leaders, it is about replacing them fast and ensuring that the new cohort of leaders is ready to deal with a world that is characterized by digital disruption, uncertainty and complexity. This new reality demands that leaders get exposure to a broader range of experiences as they climb the ladder to senior roles so that they can competently lead organizations through uncertain times. Before we take a closer look at the capabilities that leaders must be equipped with, let us first briefly explore the environment they are likely to be operating in.

## Robotics, AI and digital disruption

The future of work has already arrived, and it is spreading to new areas of our lives every day. What used to be futuristic ideas only a decade ago are now a reality. Human–robot hybrids are created through wearable exoskeletons and 3D printing is transforming manufacturing.[17] Autonomous cars are driving on our roads and algorithms are making sentencing decisions and are setting bail terms in some US states by working out the likelihood that someone will reoffend.[18] Retailers allow algorithms that can predict what customers will buy within the next 30 days to automatically order merchandise from third-party suppliers without human input into the decision-making process.[19]

In a survey of over 350 AI experts and developers conducted by Oxford University and Yale University, the consensus indicated a 50 per cent chance that by 2060, in about 40 years' time, machines will be better than humans in all tasks.[20] Predictions put AI's mastery of translating language, writing high-school essays and driving trucks within less than 10 years. And by 2049, AI will be writing bestselling novels and 4 years later it will have mastered surgery. The predictions go on to state that within the next 120 years all human jobs will be automated.

Furthermore, the digital economy is growing fast and predicted to grow to 25 per cent of the world's economy by 2020.[21] This part of the economy is driven by unprecedented connectivity and characterized by phenomena such as social networks, the use of mobile access to the internet and smart devices connected through the internet of things.[22] In 2014, IBM estimated that we generate 2.5 quintillion bytes of data every day from a wide range of different sources, such as physical sensors, social media posts, digital photos, various forms of communication and much else.[23]

Organizations across many different industry sectors, particularly so in customer-facing industries such as media, telecoms and customer finance, are being disrupted by the increasing digitalization of the workplace.[24, 25] This means that organizations must provide outstanding digital experiences to both customers and employees who are getting used to engaging and easy-to-use solutions from new, disruptive start-ups. Using big data to help customers get the best possible customer service or shopping experience is core to staying competitive.[26] It also means that organizations must create environments that foster collaboration within the organization as well as beyond, including in some cases collaboration with competitors. Collaboration increases agility, innovation and the ability to respond fast to customer demands. Furthermore, organizations must adapt their business models, supply chain and the skills set of their employees to help them stay ahead of the competition.[27]

While change has long been a feature of organizational life, the pace of disruption will increase. Some 86 per cent of executives expect that the pace of technological change brought to their industries by digitalization will continue to accelerate.[28]

## The VUCA world

In the context of this rapid technological change, the world is sometimes described as VUCA: volatile, uncertain, complex and ambiguous.[29] These characteristics add further demands to a leader's list of challenges to be mastered. In *volatile* situations, leaders must deal with unexpected events such as price volatility after a natural disaster or the market entrance of a disruptive new competitor. In *uncertain* situations, leaders encounter situations that make planning difficult. Some have talked about *radical uncertainty*, particularly so in relation to political disruption where unforeseen political outcomes create extreme uncertainty such as the outcomes of the Brexit referendum and the US presidential election in 2016, or the French and UK general elections in 2017.[30] Radical uncertainty means that it is hard to predict the future. What has worked in the past no longer seems to hold true.

*Complexity* is created by an interconnected, global business world where organizations may be doing business across many different geographies with many different tariffs, or where decisions are increasingly based on advanced algorithms. This means that leaders must be able to develop expertise in new areas fast. And technological changes not only increase complexity, they also create significant disruption. This disruption creates *ambiguity* where new technologies and new markets mean that we don't yet understand what will and what won't work. As a result, leaders must experiment and try new approaches to gain a better understanding of the situation.

## Capabilities for tomorrow's leaders

> Leaders play an important role when it comes to change and determining future success. Good leadership is no longer part of a high-potential's basic education – it has become a strategic differentiator.
>
> Torsten Schmeichel, former Head of People Development, Global
> Microelectronics Organization

Clearly, today's and tomorrow's leaders are not short of challenges. Leadership skills such as 'commons creating', 'smart mob organizing' and 'rapid prototyping' have been proposed as ways to deal with the ongoing innovation and rapid disruption leaders are likely to encounter.[31] As before though, leaders still require some fundamental leadership qualities, as can be seen in Figure 1.1, that continue to hold currency in a VUCA world, and may even have become more important as a result of it.

**Figure 1.1**    Leadership qualities for the VUCA world

| | |
|---|---|
| Emotional intelligence, vulnerability and humbleness | 01 |

| | |
|---|---|
| 02 | Inspirational communication |

| | |
|---|---|
| Openness to change and comfort with ambiguity | 03 |

| | |
|---|---|
| 04 | Embracing risk |

| | |
|---|---|
| Curiosity and fast learner | 05 |

| | |
|---|---|
| 06 | Reflection, developing self and others |

| | |
|---|---|
| Collaboration, co-creation and trust | 07 |

| | |
|---|---|
| 08 | Accountability |

## *Emotionally intelligent and human leaders who inspire*

> To enable and empower your team to be more than the sum of their parts, you need to create a compelling vision they want to get behind; a clear plan they understand their part in; and a culture they want to be a part of. Getting this right at the outset – and throughout the journey – is the most important place to invest your time.
>
> Bella Vuillermoz, Director, Property Service Group, Sky UK

Not surprisingly, emotional intelligence is a key attribute of a leader in the VUCA world. It is about leadership in its most basic form: getting people to follow a leader in a world that is unpredictable and often uncomfortable as it lacks clarity. Leaders must inspire others with their vision for the future, with their plans for organizational transformations and with the way ahead in times of turmoil and volatility. Mature and emotionally aware leaders who are willing to show vulnerability and are able to share stories of overcoming personal challenges and setbacks will be more effective at engaging others.

Leaders who are able to recognize and respond to the personal anxieties caused by organizational transformations, and who share their personal belief that the organization is able to overcome any impeding obstacles, are more likely to create joint ownership for difficult challenges ahead.

## Openness to change, ambiguity and risk

We have already seen how important it is for leaders to inspire in moments of uncertainty and transformation. To do this well, a leader must first embrace the uncertainty and any impending change themselves. They must be ready to move out of their comfort zone and take risks with unfamiliar roles or yet unproven ventures. Uncertainties must become opportunities, and to fully harness these, an emerging leader requires mobility and flexibility. This flexibility can be as simple as being able to move from being a functional expert on one project to being the project leader on the next project. Roles are predicted to become more fluid. It may also mean that from a career point of view, the leader takes opportunities presented by volatile markets and makes the most of these. Market volatility may mean that the only strategically important roles available are to close a production site or to divest a part of a business. While this may not be the high-potential employee's favourite role, they must be ready to take on this role as it represents an important learning opportunity. Successful leaders are ready to take on a broad range of challenges that allow them to experience different stages of an organization's growth cycle: starting something new, growing it, working abroad and delivering successfully across cultures, transformation, and turnaround and rejuvenation.

## Curiosity and wanting to learn more

In the VUCA world knowledge moves fast and while there is no need to develop deep technical expertise in new domains, there is nevertheless the need to stay curious and understand how new developments may help or hinder the success of their organizations. As a result, leaders must be ready to learn continuously.

## Reflective learning

This curiosity about the external world must also be mirrored in the leaders' desire to learn about themselves. Reflecting about their own behaviours and interactions with others allows leaders to focus on continuous self-improvement. Furthermore, successful leaders gather feedback and review situations with peers and clients for business improvement. A leader cannot make the same mistake twice. Good leaders extend this critical path of learning and growth to their teams and make time for career and development conversations with their direct reports. Leaders must build knowledge in themselves, their teams and the organization as a whole.

## Collaborate, co-create and be trusted

In times of fast technological advances, where different trends such as machine learning, robotics and digitalization collide to create new threats and opportunities, leaders must be able to inspire trust in others and create environments where people can collaborate and co-create new solutions and products. Allowing others to experiment, fail and try again is vital in a world where innovation and disruption is a key differentiator. In these situations, technical skills are only a base layer. Leaders must be true to their word and accept failure as the price for innovation. Only then will employees be ready to experiment, innovate and not fear failure. Furthermore, for true collaboration to take place, leaders benefit from a less directive and a more inclusive leadership style. This helps to create an environment where people from different backgrounds can come together, where all ideas count and where everyone can work to the best of their abilities.

## Accountability

Accountability matters more than ever in uncertain and volatile situations. It is about taking accountability for delivering results and seeing opportunities rather than blaming turbulent market conditions for disappointing results. Organizations require leaders who face and own the uncertainty and volatility of markets. Accountability is also closely related to the need for innovation and taking risks. Leaders must be willing to accept ultimate responsibility for failure in the quest for innovation and trying new things. Accountability will not only be important for the most senior of leaders. As organizations move to more flexible project-working where accountability and decision-making are passed down the organizational hierarchy, everyone must be ready to be accountable.

## In practice: the importance of leadership in the VUCA world

Leadership development is critical. Some people look at leadership development as a training programme for the top tier. We are trying to promote that everyone should demonstrate leadership. We are encouraging everyone to take the lead and to improve in their role. For senior people and those with responsibility for other people, we want to create a climate where people feel empowered, motivated and cared for. Some people have a natural ability to motivate; for others with people-management responsibility it is not natural, so we are trying to help and support them.

Brian Callaghan, Global Head of Leadership Development,
Executive Resourcing & Corporate University, Global Steel &
Mining Organization

Leadership is very important. Young people whom we want to attract to our organization no longer want to work in old hierarchies. Leadership is also important to help us as an organization to deal with disruption. The leader of the future sees mobility and flexibility as an opportunity. We must be able to move people from functional expertise to project-based work. People must be able to deal with shifts in role and responsibility: sometimes you are the expert, then the boss, then you are a colleague. We need adaptability.

Dr Ursula Schütze-Kreilkamp, Head of Group HR Development &
Group Executives, Deutsche Bahn AG

> I personally believe that leadership development is key to the future
> of our business success. Our business is only as good as its people.
> We have to adjust to customers and anticipate market circumstances.
> Leaders help our organization to facilitate important change and we
> must help our people to help the organization.
>
> Robert Baker, Senior Partner, Mercer

# What does this mean for leadership development?

To meet the demand for leadership talent, be this business, functional or technical leaders, organizations must develop their top talent at increased speed. In Chapter 2, we will explore what this means in terms of actual years to the top of an organization, the percentage of time that can be taken off a career journey to a senior role, as well as the average time in the role. Acceleration is potentially a resource-intensive endeavour as it means paying full attention to an employee and charting out the most effective career path for this person. Organizations must therefore find ways of delivering a self-service offering for the majority of employees, which will free up budget and time for a small number of carefully selected high-potential employees. We will explore the role of career management as the foundation for accelerated leadership development in Chapter 2.

Emerging leaders must have worked in a range of environments and learned how to deliver results in a variety of challenging situations. This means that both high-potential employees as well as organizations must understand what type of roles and stretch assignments are best suited to provide these varied experiences. We will look at the most developmental stretch assignments in Chapter 3. Furthermore, organizations must find affordable and effective solutions to provide these experiences to their pool of carefully selected high-potential employees. In Chapter 4, we will explore the programmes and development solutions that organizations employ to give their top talent access to the necessary stretch roles.

Each new assignment brings with it new challenges and an increased risk of failure, either in the form of personal derailment or as a costly business mistake. At the heart of an accelerated development philosophy lies the concept of stretch; moving a person out of their comfort zone and into high-visibility roles for which they don't yet have all the necessary skills and knowledge. As a result, organizations must be willing to take risks on high-potential employees, but it is likely that this creates a conflict between appointing a tried and tested candidate versus a candidate who has yet to learn the ropes. In Chapter 5, we will examine the dark side of acceleration and how to guard against personal derailment, and in Chapter 6 we will explore the steps that organizations can take to fully embrace a development approach that carries additional organizational risks.

It is not the experience itself but the learning that a high-potential employee extracts from it that creates learning. Without the willingness to learn from feedback and to personally reflect on past experiences, a leader is likely to make the same mistakes again and fail to adapt adequately to new situations. Encouraging personal reflection in an action-orientated world comes with several challenges. In Chapter 7, we will explore the importance of reflection and how to make it happen in a busy workplace. Chapter 8 analyses the importance of creating support networks for accelerated leaders through people such as managers, mentors and coaches.

Finally, a one-size-fits-all approach is rarely as effective as a personalized solution. However, to achieve economies of scale, organizations must develop programmes for their dedicated talent pools, which will allow them to give more people access to leadership development. In Chapters 9 and 10, we will look at how accelerated leadership development can be made to work for two key talent pools, millennials and women. Millennials *want* accelerated leadership development but often don't get ready access to it, just like women who *need* accelerated leadership development. We will delve into the additional barriers and biases that organizations must overcome to make accelerated leadership development programmes work at scale.

As we will see throughout the remainder of this book, accelerated leadership development contains seven key elements, as shown in Figure 1.2:

**Figure 1.2**   The seven-step model of accelerated leadership development

- identifying and assessing leadership potential;
- providing a breadth of job experiences;
- an appetite for risk-taking both by high-potential employees and their organizations;
- developing through on-the-job learning;
- providing consolidation phases;
- a willingness to reflect and actively extract learning from past experiences;
- access to various sources of support while on an accelerated career path.

## Summary

Leaders are key to organizational success and at a time when many are retiring, a new cohort of leaders must be developed fast to take their place. This new cohort of leaders, however, must be equipped to deal with a world that is characterized by volatility, uncertainty, complexity and ambiguity – in short, the VUCA world. In this world, the unprecedented speed of technological change, digital disruption and the advent of machine learning and AI means that to successfully lead a business, or part of it, leaders must have experienced a range of different challenges and have worked in a variety of roles to prepare for the challenges they are likely to encounter.

Many organizations are already expressing concerns about the capabilities of their current leaders to lead their organizations successfully into the future. Furthermore, the very group of people from which organizations will draw this new generation of leaders, the millennials, are hungry for development and fast progression. Organizations that do not take active steps to provide accelerated development will lose their most capable young talent to competitors.

The new cohort of leaders requires a range of leadership capabilities, ranging from emotional intelligence, inspirational communication and curiosity to reflection, collaboration and co-creation.

To develop well-rounded leaders fast, organizations must be clear about the types of roles and stretch assignments that are most developmental for these future leaders. They must also put in place organizational programmes and processes to take leaders through such experiences. Recognizing early warning signs of potential derailment of accelerated leaders as well as instilling a culture that enables acceleration are two areas for organizations to focus on. Development support from others, such as managers and mentors, and personal reflection help to maximize the learning that a leader can extract from each experience. Finally, to ensure that programmes work effectively for the intended target group, organizations must be mindful of additional challenges for talent pools such as millennials or women.

## Organizational design tips

- **Develop a business case for acceleration**. Secure the longevity of your acceleration programme by developing a strong business case for acceleration. Any successful acceleration programme must be linked to your organization's business strategy. Use company-specific data where available to build your arguments rather than relying on generic data and arguments, which tend to be less persuasive. Once developed, communicate widely and actively engage senior leaders and key stakeholders to obtain buy-in.

- **Forecast your leadership requirements**. As part of your succession planning, project the organization's need for future leaders across the business to gain a better understanding of the extent of acceleration that you require. Evaluate historic data, such as hiring, retention, turnover and progression data as a basis for this projection.

- **Review your definitions of leadership**. Ensure that your leadership competencies reflect the reality of the VUCA world where capabilities such as openness to ambiguity, co-creation and reflective learning are core requirements for successful leaders. Technical skills will no longer be a differentiator.

- **Review your current leadership development solutions**. All data points to the importance of good leadership. With increased disruption and volatility, this is unlikely to change. Develop a clear strategy for leadership development and review existing solutions for their effectiveness of developing holistic leaders who thrive in an uncertain and complex world. MBA courses and classroom learning are unlikely to help leaders learn how to innovate and deal with radical uncertainty where no rules of how to solve problems exist yet.

## Individual coaching tips

- **Embrace change and uncertainty**. Change is often difficult to deal with. It creates uncertainty and anxiety. We often dislike change and the lack of certainty that stems from it. Find ways of getting comfortable, or more comfortable, in situations of change and ambiguity as it represents the new normal.

- **Don't neglect emotional intelligence in a technology-driven world**. The pace of change and the impact of potential disruptions mean that emerging leaders must be able to inspire others: to find courage in difficult times, to buy into visions of the future or to deliver outstanding results. Emotional intelligence will help you understand other people's emotions as well as your impact on others' emotions. It is an important, yet sometimes difficult, skill to develop. If you find it difficult, persevere. It will pay off.

- **Curiosity**. Stay curious about technological advances and new developments. At the same time, make space to learn about yourself, your actions and what you could do differently next time. Reflection will provide you with important insights, increased self-awareness and the ability to learn faster.

# Notes

**1** Wang, G, Oh, I-S, Courtright, SH and Colbert, AE (2011) Transformational Leadership and Performance Across Criteria and Levels: A meta-analytic review of 25 years of research, *Group & Organization Management*, **36**, pp 223–70

**2** Inceoglu, I, Thomas, G, Chu, C, Plans, D and Gerbasi, A (in press) Leadership behavior and employee well-being: An integrated review and a future research agenda, *Leadership Quarterly*

**3** Wang, G, Oh, I-S, Courtright, SH and Colbert, AE (2011) Transformational Leadership and Performance Across Criteria and Levels: A meta-analytic review of 25 years of research, *Group & Organization Management*, **36**, pp 223–70

**4** The Institute of Leadership & Management (2014) *Talent Pipeline*, available from www.InstituteLM.com/resourceLibrary/TalentPipeline. html

**5** Loew, L (2015) *State of Leadership Development 2015: The time to act is now*, Brandon Hall Group

**6** Human Capital Institute (2014) *How to Accelerate Leadership Development*, in partnership with UNC Kenan-Flagler Business School

**7** Tossi, M (2012) *Labor Force Projections to 2020: A more slowly growing workforce,* Bureau of Labor Statistics, downloaded at: https://www.bls.gov/opub/mlr/2012/01/art3full.pdf (last accessed 27 January 2018)

**8** United Nations Department of Economic and Social Affairs (2013) *World Population Ageing*

**9** European Commission (2014) *The 2015 Ageing Report*

**10** Dobbs, R, Madgavkar, A, Barton, D, Labaye, E,  Manyika, J, Roxburgh, C, Lund, S and Madhav, S (2012) *The World at Work: Jobs, pay, and skills for 3.5 billion people*, McKinsey Global Institute, June 2012

**11** Dobbs, R,  Remes, J,  Manyika, J, Roxburgh, C, Smit, S and Schaer, F (2012) *Urban World: Cities and the rise of the consuming class,* McKinsey Global Institute, June 2012

**12** Economist Intelligence Unit (2010) *Global Firms in 2020: The next decade of change for organisations and workers*, Economist Intelligence Unit Limited

**13** Deloitte (2016) *The 2016 Deloitte Millennial Survey*

**14** Institute of Employment Studies (2004) *The Drivers of Employee Engagement*

**15** PwC (2011) Millennials at Work. Reshaping the workplace

**16** IBM (2015) Myths, Exaggerations and Uncomfortable Truths: The real story behind millennials

**17** Dr Ashitey Trebi-Ollennu, chief engineer at Nasa's Jet Propulsion Laboratory

**18** Reynolds, M (2017) Bias test to keep algorithms ethical, *New Scientist*, 1 April 2017

**19** *The Economist* (2017) Automatic for the people, 15 April 2017

**20** Quoted in *New Scientist*, 10 June 2017

**21** Accenture (2016) Digital Economic Value Index quoted in People first: The primacy of people in a digital age, *Accenture Technology Vision*, January 2016

**22** Gada, K (2016) The Digital Economy in 5 Minutes, *Forbes*, 16 June 2016

**23** https://www-01.ibm.com/software/in/data/bigdata/

**24** Grossman, R (2016) The industries that are being disrupted the most by digital, *Harvard Business Review*, 21 March 2016

**25** Bundesministerium für Arbeit und Soziales, Germany, *Arbeiten 4.0*, Arbeit Weiterdenken, Grünbuch, http://www.bmas.de/SharedDocs/Downloads/DE/PDF-Publikationen-DinA4/gruenbuch-arbeiten-vier-null.pdf?__blob=publicationFile

**26** Anderson, L and Wladawsky-Berger, I (2016) The four things it takes to succeed in the digital economy, *Harvard Business Review*, 24 March 2016

**27** Accenture Technology Vision (2016) People First: The Primacy of People in a Digital Age

**28** Accenture Technology Vision (2016) People First: The Primacy of People in a Digital Age

**29** Bennett, N and Lemoine, GJ (2014) What VUCA really means for you, *Harvard Business Review*, Jan/Feb 2014

**30** Münchau, W (2017) Welcome to the age of radical uncertainty, *Financial Times*, 19 June 2017

**31** Johansen, R (2012) *Leaders Make the Future: Ten new leadership skills for an uncertain world*, Berrett-Koehler, San Francisco, CA

# Moving at pace  02
## The speed of leaders

*High flyers have always been promoted more quickly. We must now achieve this with more people so that we are not falling behind. We can no longer wait. We need organizational structures in place that allow us to accomplish this acceleration.*

DR URSULA SCHÜTZE-KREILKAMP, HEAD OF GROUP HR
DEVELOPMENT & GROUP EXECUTIVES, DEUTSCHE BAHN AG

*If you want to get all the way to the top, to board level, then you have to move fast.*

MATTHIAS METZGER, GLOBAL HEAD OF TALENT MANAGEMENT &
ORGANIZATIONAL DEVELOPMENT, CONTINENTAL AG

## The speed of leaders

As we saw in Chapter 1, there are pressing drivers that necessitate an acceleration of leadership development: the need for broad leadership skills to succeed in the VUCA world, the retirement of baby boomers, the rise of emerging countries and the desire of millennials to assume leadership roles to achieve impact and influence.

The majority of the HR leaders whom I interviewed for this book have seen their organization embrace acceleration fully. It is part and parcel of the organization's leadership development approach. In these organizations, the most promising cohort of leaders is taken through a dedicated acceleration programme. Acceleration has become the new norm.

Leaders at the top of an organization tend to get there on an accelerated track. They move faster than their former colleagues. This trend has been observed for some time.[1,2] It could be argued that leaders who make it to the top at a younger age are better leaders, as they have managed to take leadership crucibles in a shorter time. How long it takes executives to get to the top depends on the type of organization a high-potential employee works for. In a review of the CVs of top executives at Fortune 100 companies, Professors Cappelli, Hamori and Bonet found that moving to the top at a younger company such as Google takes on average 14 years, whereas it takes on average 32 years at older companies such as HP and ConocoPhillips. The average age for an executive at Google is 46, whereas at HP it is 58. While there are still far fewer women than men in the most senior roles, data suggests that when women do move to the very top of an organization they tend to get there faster and at a younger age than their male counterparts. We will return to the topic of women's career progression at the end of this book.[3]

## Accelerating by 25 to 30 per cent

My interview data tells a similar story. As illustrated in the In Practice box below, the average time it seems to take employees to get from graduate level to a director role, which represents the entry level for senior leadership, is about 7 to 10 years. Moving from graduate level to senior executive level, which is one level below the CEO and his or her team, seems to take about 12 to 15 years. And the move to C-level tends to take about 20 years in large corporations. While these numbers vary somewhat depending on the size and industry sector of the organization, there is broad agreement that these trajectories can be reduced by between 25 and 30 per cent, provided four key factors are in place:

1 the accelerated leader has the right 'raw material': intellect, drive and being an agile learner;

2 access to the right roles;

3 access to the right support network;

4 being spotted and fostered as talent early.

We will explore each of these factors in more detail as we progress through the book.

## In practice: accelerating leadership development journeys

We are exploring how to accelerate the careers of employees, especially those considered to be high-potential and future senior leaders. We recognize the need to mutually agree how we intensify development experiences. This is vital if we are going to be successful again at appointing another internal CEO in their early 40s. Instead of doing one job in two to three years, we are planning shorter tenure in some roles and ensuring our high-potential employees are in the critical roles that the organization has identified. This approach will build breadth, new capabilities and complementary perspectives. While the career paths will be crafted on a case by case basis, it means greater stretch between roles and fewer incremental moves. The employee and the organization will take more calculated risks.

Kim Lafferty, VP People Development, GlaxoSmithKline

Yes, you can accelerate development. You could potentially reduce from 10 years to 7 years or less. But to do this, you need the right locus of control, drive and intellect. People are capable of achieving great things if you put them in the right role and give them the right motivation and support. Experience can count for a lot, but too much of it might lead to entrenched perspectives that could impair performance.

David Clarke, Global Head of People Capability,
Syngenta International

From entry to senior management level takes about 15 years. You can only reduce this through networking and changing company. Many people underestimate the importance of networking. Networking allows you to be put forward for the right jobs. Most of our stretch assignments are roles with a lot of visibility. If a stretch assignment is not important for a key decision-maker in the organization, then it doesn't carry much weight. It is important to be noticed so when key roles come up, people remember you.

Alexandra Aubart, Director Organizational
Development, LSG Lufthansa Service Holding AG

From graduate level to C-level it takes on average 20 years. And from graduate to director level normally takes 10 years, but we can reduce this by 30 per cent. There are some pockets of excellence where we have promoted people to director level within 7 years. These are people whose talent we spotted and developed early on in their careers.

Jo Hindle, Head of HR Asset Services, EMEA, Cushman & Wakefield

You need two to three years in a role. Three years is more realistic than two years. To leave your mark with a role, two to three years is a good period. We have guidelines with regards to someone staying in a role for too long, but this is sometimes difficult to adhere to if someone is a good performer and if they are happy to stay where they are. We must be mindful that this can become a blocker for follow-up talent. If someone stays in role for more than three to four years, then we make this transparent.

Matthias Kempf, former Vice President Human Resources Emerging Markets, The adidas Group

If you move too soon then it looks like you cannot stick at anything. When I hire people and see that a candidate is a serial butterfly, then I am careful. However, a few short stints don't bother me. Long stints bother me more; if you are too comfortable you don't push yourself and you don't perform.

Rachel Gray, Sales Director, Experian plc

## Add a year in role for each management level

There seems to be an expectation that employees stay in a junior role for 12 to 18 months; at mid-management level this moves up to two to three years; and at senior management level, it is on average three to four years. The length of time in role is also driven by the availability of new roles. Where employees are not mobile enough to move geographically for a role, they may not be able to move up.

Staying in a role for two or three years brings additional advantages such as ensuring that business benefits have been delivered and that knowledge has been built within a team. It also allows the high-potential employee to experience the impact of their own decisions. Furthermore, moving to a new role faster than every two years may increase the risk of burnout and if a high-potential employee moves to a new employer every two to three years, doubts may be raised about their grit and how easy it is to work with them. We will come back to the danger of burnout and of not getting the opportunity to experience the impact of one's decisions in the next chapter.

## 3–5–7 and 3 x 3

The 3–5–7 rule is a golden tenure rule for our senior teams. They should be in role for a minimum of three years, five years is ideal, and seven years is maximum. This creates stability for the team, for customers and for the organization during transformations. You can also learn to live with the impact of your mistakes. If you keep moving on after 12 to 18 months there is instability and unrest.

Catalina Schveninger, Global Head of Resourcing & Employer Brand, Vodafone

With a focus on increasing breadth, some organizations are now setting a maximum level for time in role, although there seems to be some disagreement about how long is too long. While some organizations set the limit at five years and argue that performance, culture and breadth of experience are impacted if people stay in role longer than five years, others insist that five years is an ideal period and that it is the seven-year mark instead when someone has stayed in role too long. These organizations follow a slower path: the 3–5–7 path. This means that they expect a person to be in role for at least three years, ideally five years and anything over seven years is deemed as too long. For some organizations this rule applies to their senior team, for others it applies to technical roles where a person is expected to go through an entire product cycle to learn about all the nuances and aspects of it before they are deemed ready to move on. The rationale for setting five years as the ideal time is a concern that too much change-over in leaders, particularly at the top of the organization or in key technical roles, creates too much unrest and disruption for direct reports and clients, which means that results are likely to suffer.

One formula for acceleration that a few of the interviewees mentioned as a guiding principle for emerging talent is the 3 x 3 approach that refers to three years at each of the following three levels:

- leading self;
- leading people;
- leading leaders.

**Figure 2.1**   Accelerated leadership development in numbers

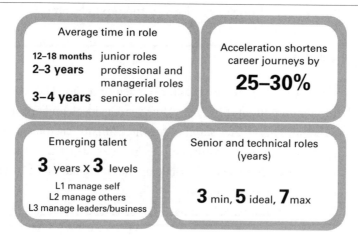

As a next step, the high-potential employee moves to leading a business. In some organizations, the third level already refers to leading a business, thus representing an even steeper acceleration. The first year of the three-year period is spent learning the role, the second year is about instigating change and delivering results. The third year allows for consolidation and dealing with the consequences of decisions and actions taken in the previous two years.

Figure 2.1 summarizes these various formulae for accelerated development.

## Breadth as an accelerator

How do organizations achieve this acceleration? At its most fundamental level, the concept of acceleration is intrinsically bound up with the concept of breadth, which is a high-potential employee's exposure to different types of experiences and roles to help them get ready to deal with the challenges they will face as a leader. To enable acceleration, we must help a high-potential employee gain this breadth of experience in the shortest possible time.

A study of CVs of the Fortune 100's top leaders has shown that those who move to the top are less likely to have spent their entire career at the same organization. This is particularly the case for organizations that have undergone significant restructuring due to external market pressures. These organizations are more likely to hire senior executives from outside rather than promoting internal talent, which is a more likely route to the top in more stable organizations. Getting to the very top demands a varied background. While all careers benefit from diversity in experience and from having moved across functions, this is particularly the case for top executives. Those at the upper echelons of an organization had roles in different functions or business units, including operational roles.[4]

Another study, this time of 459,000 LinkedIn profiles, also shows that functional diversity pays off. Those who have held roles in different functions such as marketing, finance, operations or HR, are significantly more likely to become a senior executive. Moving firms doesn't seem to make much difference, whereas moving across industries somewhat reduces the likelihood of moving to the top.[5]

Breadth allows leaders to develop agility and the ability to deal with volatility and continued change. Being exposed to a range of roles enables leaders to build broad networks in an organization, obtain an organization-wide perspective and learn to adapt their work approach and problem-solving style to different situations. It helps to move a future leader away from technical expertise and instead focuses the person on business drivers. As a result, a core element of acceleration programmes is the focus on consciously broadening out a future leader's experience base.

In research that I conducted while still at IBM, I repeatedly found, in three separate studies, that having a broader set of job experiences, such as building something from scratch, turning around a failing project or managing a team, was the strongest predictor of gaining a promotion. We will explore the different types of experiences that leaders must gain exposure to in Chapter 3, and in Chapter 4, we will see how organizations incorporate conscious broadening out in their leadership development programmes. In Chapter 9, we will come back to the IBM study and further delve into its findings in relation to women's careers.

# The time–cost–quality equation

> There is a time–cost–quality equation. If you spend millions you can develop high-quality leaders in a short period of time. The real question is, how can you consistently accelerate the development of leaders within the normal financial constraints of most organizations?
>
> David Clarke, Global Head of People Capability,
> Syngenta International

The time–cost–quality equation points to the constraints that organizations must work within. A fourth dimension to consider is 'scope'. In the case of accelerated leadership development this refers to the number of high-potential employees who can be accelerated in their leadership development journey. For accelerated leadership development, the time component is fixed. The very essence of accelerated leadership development demands that we spend as little time as possible on the development of leaders. As we saw earlier in this chapter, the aim is to reduce an unaided career journey by 25 to 30 per cent, a significant reduction.

Accelerating the development of high-potential employees into high-quality, well-rounded leaders who can successfully take the reins of a technical area, a function or an entire organization, is potentially a resource-intensive process. It requires the time of HR professionals and line managers who assess a person's potential and collect feedback on their performance. Furthermore, HR professionals and managers must help devise development plans, secure development opportunities and stay close to an emerging leader to ensure that the high-potential employee is always stretched in their role, that learning and development take place and that support is available should the high-potential employee struggle in their demanding role. Moreover, it takes senior mentors to provide visibility and access to challenging roles and coaches to encourage reflection and increased self-awareness.

No organization can afford this much input for every talented employee in the organization. As a result, organizations must find a way to provide a more resource-efficient solution that can cover a much larger number of employees. Career management seems to be the solution that organizations are relying on.

# Career management: laying the foundation for organization-wide acceleration

> If we have no career management, then I have assets in the organization that I am not working well. You have wasted talent if they are not doing what they are meant to do and if we don't point them in the right direction.
>
> Dr Siobhan Martin, Executive Director UK HR, Mercer

Careers are sometimes described as 'boundaryless' or 'protean' as a reflection of the fact that careers are now much more driven by individuals who take responsibility for developing their skills to stay relevant and employable.[6, 7] As knowledge workers, they offer their talents to several different organizations. Therefore, careers are often defined as 'a process along a path of experience and jobs that may be in one or more organizations'.[8] Career management helps individuals chart the most effective path of experiences and jobs. By being clear about what they want to achieve, employees are more focused on taking roles and joining organizations that help them get closer to their goal. However, career goals may change along the way and it is important to keep options open in a world that is characterized by constant change.

To develop talent at scale, organizations are relying on high-potential employees' self-initiative to manage their own careers, as can be seen in the In Practice box below. While organizations differ in the level of support they are offering their employees, every HR and business leader I interviewed agreed that career management must be the responsibility of the individual. As part of this self-management approach, employees must find the motivation to work out their career goals and find strategies to help them achieve these goals. They must also be ready to stay flexible with regards to their career options. The VUCA world is likely to bring rapid and repeated change for a high-potential employee's career.

Organizations also struggle with this change. Investments in long-term career plans for individuals or detailed organizational career maps may not pay off as industry volatility or organizational restructuring can quickly make them irrelevant.

## In practice: organizations' career management expectations and practices

Career management is a main focus for us. That's why we are using 360-degree feedback. The classic career management model is outdated. It is no longer important what somebody achieves but how they achieve it – you cannot leave scorched earth behind. We are moving our focus towards customer orientation and innovation. We need a trust-based and caring culture and we need to define how we interact with each other. These values are reflected in our newly defined leadership principles and we expect all our employees to meet these. Our leaders need to be capable of handling uncertainty and to master the VUCA world. We also want our leaders to promote and develop the career of others.

Ursula Schwarzenbart, Head of Talent Development &
Diversity Management, Daimler AG

We have just launched a career framework: Explore. Evaluate. Engage. We put the accountability and control of career management in the hands of the individual. We are clear – we are here to support, and you need to be proactive and accountable. We will provide the tools and be clear about what we expect from you. And we will be transparent and provide information and feedback. With this new framework we are moving from a career ladder to a career spider web. If someone hasn't done a certain type of job before, then we show how they can get there. We need to give people support at the beginning. We also need to address how we relate to failure. We are really aiming to change mindsets. I believe in resilience. We are providing large-scale webinars to all employees and managers to educate them about the framework. Managers often don't know how to have career conversations with employees. Often these conversations are a coaching situation and there is power in strong questions. The framework will help us to drive performance management. We want to evolve performance management to incentivize development.

Selina Millstam, Vice President & Global Head
of Talent Management, Ericsson

We strongly believe that the employee is in charge of their own career. We ask our employees to drive their career and their development, to engage in open dialogue and to get feedback and to reflect. This helps them see how others perceive them. It helps answer questions like: 'Where am I now? Where do I want to go?' We then match this with an organizational perspective, funnelling into active succession management and career paths. The world around us and the expectations of our employees are constantly changing. So the sweet spot lies in matching an employee's ambitions and their learning agility and curiosity with what the organization needs.

Vera Gramkow, Global Head of Talent & Performance Development, Bayer AG

Career management is essential but there are so many unwritten rules. We have developed a framework so that people know what is expected. There are three things. First, what are you good at? Second, what are you passionate about? And finally, what does the company need you to do? If you draw it as a Venn diagram, the spot in the middle is the sweet spot. We must work out what on-the-job experiences you need to move to the next level. There is an element of ownership. We develop the tools to support you, but you need to own your career development.

Rachel Osikoya, Head of Diversity & Inclusion, Global Transportation & Logistics Organization

For 'My Development' we created a framework, a ladder that points out various career steps and career paths. We positioned it as a personal journey. It is positioned as a jungle gym so you go up, and down, too. We want to make employees more accountable for their careers. The framework allows them to ask questions: 'Where do I want to be in the short, medium and long term?' It helps you have conversations with your supervisor and it provides competencies. We have used the framework in a D&I [Diversity & Inclusion] context, too. The framework helps employees access relevant training in the training catalogue. The framework introduces the 70:20:10 model and provides employees with a lot of information about what they could do as on-the-job development opportunities. It also allows you to log your development activities.

Raquel Montejo, Assistant Director, Learning & Development, IATA

The HR leaders that I interviewed referred to a host of career resources that employees have access to, such as:

- Career information in the form of career frameworks, maps and/ or personal career stories. Furthermore, organizations advertise available roles.

- Development content in the form of curated information on the internet, in-house e-learning programmes or formal training courses.

- Personalized development conversations and development plans.

- Formal, organization-wide succession planning approaches as well as the formal assessment of potential through psychometric tests and the assessment of current performance through feedback.

- Career development conversations with HR experts and with line managers.

In return, organizations expect individual employees to drive their own career, which involves identifying their own career goals, as well as identifying available opportunities and taking the initiative to put themselves forward for these opportunities. There is an expectation that personal development will happen largely through self-service of available e-learning, as can be seen in Figure 2.2.

## The deal and the virtuous cycle

Organizations must, however, create a virtuous cycle where a high-potential employee's career self-management efforts are met with increased access to more formal development. Otherwise, the risk of high-potential talent leaving is significantly increased.[9] Many organizations still seem to recognize this principle. Those high-potential employees who have shown motivation and initiative to drive their own career progression, along with having delivered expected business results, tend to be selected for more formal development opportunities. Furthermore, despite a decrease in organizations' commitment to their employees' career development over the past 30 to 40 years, there still seems to be an unspoken, high-level deal between organizations and their employees about working hard for the organization in exchange for career opportunities. While today's deal no longer

**Figure 2.2**   Career self-management

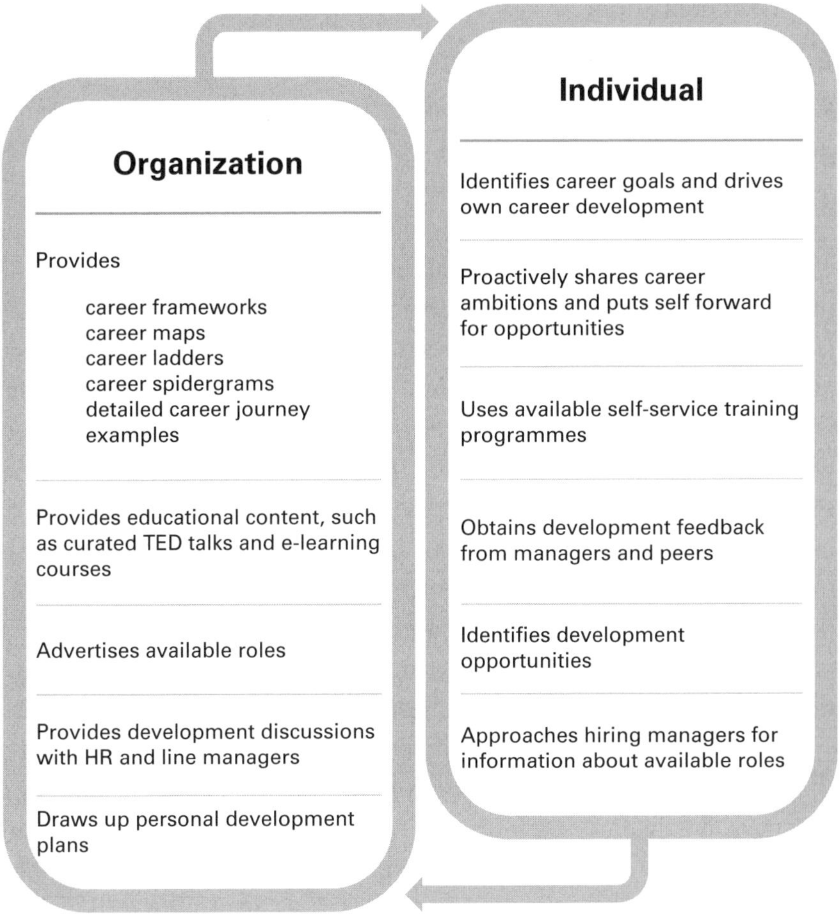

**Organization**

Provides

    career frameworks
    career maps
    career ladders
    career spidergrams
    detailed career journey
    examples

Provides educational content, such as curated TED talks and e-learning courses

Advertises available roles

Provides development discussions with HR and line managers

Draws up personal development plans

**Individual**

Identifies career goals and drives own career development

Proactively shares career ambitions and puts self forward for opportunities

Uses available self-service training programmes

Obtains development feedback from managers and peers

Identifies development opportunities

Approaches hiring managers for information about available roles

includes a career for life or guaranteed promotion prospects, there is still a recognition that development and personal growth is a key engagement driver for many employees.

## Career management practices

In an in-depth study of just under 200 organizations in the UK, Baruch and Peiperl (2000) found that the six most common career management practices were:

**1** job postings;

**2** formal education;

**3** performance appraisal for career planning;

**4** career counselling by managers;

**5** lateral moves;

**6** career counselling by HR.

These are fairly similar to the career management solutions that the interviewees talked about. Baruch and Peiperl also included practices such as succession planning, assessment centres and performance appraisals from peers and direct reports. While these have been shown to be among the most effective practices in empirical studies, they were reported less frequently. In the study for this book, these more advanced practices were typically mentioned in connection with dedicated leadership development programmes or succession planning rather than career management. This may not be surprising as the interviewees clearly defined career management as something that is driven largely by the employee, thus reflecting a more basic definition of career management than that adopted by Baruch and Peiperl.

Baruch and Peiperl identified five clusters in the 17 techniques that they explored. This is a useful framework of career planning practices, particularly with regards to the flow of career-related information between the organization and the individual employee: The five clusters are:

- *Basic*: Characterized by facilitation of employees' careers at a fundamental level, including job postings, formal education and cross-functional moves to broaden experience. These offerings are very much in line with a self-service culture – the organization provides resources, but it is up to the motivated employee to make use of them.

- *Formal*: With a focus on career plans and career ladders, and an emphasis on using books to support career planning, this cluster of career management practices contains uni-directional information exchange, flowing from the organization to the employee.

- *Active planning*: Includes performance appraisal, career counselling by the line manager and the HR department, and succession planning. These practices demonstrate the active involvement of the organization in the employee's career and do well in organizations with an open culture encourages feedback and open dialogue.

- *Active management*: Has a strong focus on bi-directional information collection and exchange between organization and employee. This cluster includes assessment centres, mentoring and career workshops.

- *Multi-directional*: Characterized by performance feedback from peers as well as direct reports, this approach collects information from multiple sources.

We will revisit the topic of career self-management in Chapter 10 when we will look at possible solutions that organizations can put in place to help younger talent develop an effective career self-management strategy.

## Summary

To get to the top requires increased speed and leaders tend to move faster than others. The interviewees agreed that compared to an 'unaided' career, accelerated careers with carefully designed development challenges and additional support can be shortened by about 25 to 30 per cent. One other clear message is that for acceleration to work, several elements need to be in place. These include a person's raw talent, access to the right roles and a supportive culture where an accelerated leader can draw on additional support to ensure that difficulties in role can be overcome and that learning takes place.

Organizations seem to be working to several different timelines to ensure that their top talent move at pace. On average, junior roles should be changed no later than two years; at middle management, job incumbents should move after two to three years; and at the top this extends to three to five years. Other guidelines are 3 x 3, which summarize the idea of moving in three-year intervals across three levels of the organization (leading self, others, managers of others).

A core ingredient of acceleration is breadth of experience. High-potential employees can only progress at increased speed if they manage to pick up this necessary breadth of experience as efficiently as possible. High-potential employees must move across functions and learn how to deal with a myriad of business challenges before they are ready to take on the reins of an organization.

To accelerate the careers of high-potential employees demands a lot of input: from managers, HR, mentors and coaches. And it is not a one-off investment but an ongoing process. Organizations must be mindful of the time–cost–quality–scope equation that determines the cost of taking a certain number of high-potential employees through an intensive acceleration process in a short period of time while guaranteeing well-rounded leaders at the end. Career management, mostly driven by employees themselves, can provide a cost-effective foundation for accelerated leadership development.

The deal that organizations strike with their employees is that the organization provides a career management framework and associated infrastructure from which motivated high-potential employees self-service. The most motivated and able who have come to the organization's attention through this process will then receive more attention. Career management practices differ across organizations in the extent to which information is exchanged between the organization and the employee. They can range from the provision of basic career management, such as job postings and career frameworks that transfer information from organization to employee, to two-way or multi-source information exchanges that include the assessment of an employee's performance and potential as well as detailed career workshops and career counselling with line managers and HR professionals.

## Organizational design tips

- **Define what acceleration means for your organization**. This may be a simple definition of the average time in role before moving on, being mindful to allow more time in a role as people become more senior and jobs more complex. Or it may be a framework such as the 3–5–7 or the 3 x 3 that we discussed. These frameworks must fit your organization and should be used as a guide rather than a strictly enforced policy.

- **Determine the unique drivers of acceleration for your organization.** Any framework, tools or processes you put in place to support accelerated leadership development must reflect career progression in your organization. Analyse data from the careers of your current leaders. What do those who moved to the top faster than others have in common? Are these criteria still relevant in the VUCA world? What are typical career blockers in your organization? Use these insights to develop an evidence-based acceleration policy and related activities, ensuring that all solutions are future-proof and don't cement the status quo.

- **Put in place the building blocks for acceleration.** Ensure that you have adequate processes and tools in place to provide the fundamentals of acceleration: a) assessing a high-potential employee's true underlying potential; b) availability of stretching and developmental roles; c) access to support systems for the accelerated leader; and d) a process that allows you to start this process early in a high-potential employee's career.

- **Provide career management foundations.** To reach as many employees as possible, build a comprehensive self-service career management offering that serves as a foundation to acceleration for all employees. Evaluate your existing offering against a framework for basic, one-way or two-way information exchange to pinpoint areas of weakness in our current offering. Those employees who show motivation and potential should receive access to more formal development programmes, thus creating a virtuous cycle.

- **Clearly communicate the organization's expectations.** While your organization's approach to career management may put the onus of career progression on the employee, make sure that these expectations are clearly communicated. A 'serve yourself' approach to career management should not turn into a 'find yourself' approach to obtaining information about available career management resources for employees. Your career management philosophy, expectations, available support and infrastructure must all be clearly communicated and easy to access. Expecting employees to self-serve with no infrastructure to self-serve from can be damaging and decrease engagement.

## Individual coaching tips

- **Demonstrate your commitment to career development.** Be proactive and don't wait for your employer to take charge of your career. It is your career and your manager will expect that you take the initiative to define your own career goals and identify opportunities. In many organizations, those who have demonstrated initiative and drive toward managing their careers are more likely to be invited to join formal development programmes. Ensure that your career stakeholders know about your career development activities.

- **Look for information.** Most organizations have information that will help you chart your career. Look for career maps or individual career journey examples, e-learning training or workshops you can attend. Alternatively, ask to meet someone more senior in your organization who has already charted a successful career to find out about their career journey. Professional institutions, such as the Association of Chartered Accountants, the British Computer Society or the American Management Association, are other good sources for typical career progression of professionals in your line of work.

- **Keep an eye on the time.** It is the results that you have delivered in role and the development you have gained that should determine whether you are ready to move on or not. Progression for the sake of progression will increase the danger of derailment and make you look too unreliable; however, it is advisable to make sure that you do not spend too long in a role once all the results have been delivered and you can no longer learn anything new. This is typically about two years in a junior role, three years in a middle management role and about four to five years in a senior role. This may vary from organization to organization and it's important to find out what your employer expects.

- **Learn about unwritten rules.** Most organizations have unwritten rules about career progression. These rules drive career progression but are not written down anywhere. It pays to get insights from a mentor or senior manager about how career progression 'works' in the organization.

# Notes

1 Cooper, CL and Cox, CJ (1979) *High Flyers: An anatomy of managerial success*, John Wiley & Sons

2 Cappelli, P, Hamori, M and Bonet, R (2014) Who's Got Those Top Jobs? *Harvard Business Review,* March 2014

3 Cappelli, P, Hamori, M and Bonet, R (2014) Who's Got Those Top Jobs? *Harvard Business Review,* March 2014

4 Cappelli, P, Hamori, M and Bonet, R (2014) Who's Got Those Top Jobs? *Harvard Business Review,* March 2014

5 Gan, L and Fritzler, A (2016) How to become an executive, LinkedIn blog, accessible at https://www.linkedin.com/pulse/how-become-executive-guy-berger-ph-d-/

6 Arthur, MB and Rousseau, DM (eds) (1996) *The Boundaryless Career*, Oxford University Press, Oxford

7 Hall, DT (1996) *The Career Is Dead: Long live the career*, Jossey-Bass, San Francisco, CA

8 Baruch and Rosenstein, 1992 as quoted on p 348 in Baruch, Y and Peiperl, M (2000) Career management practices: An empirical survey and implications, *Human Resource Management*, **39**, pp 347–66

9 Sturges, J, Guest, D, Conway, N and Mackenzie Davey, K (2002) A longitudinal study of the relationship between career management and organizational commitment among graduates in the first ten years of work, *Journal of Organizational Behavior*, **23**, pp 731–48

# Breadth of experience

# 03

## Choosing roles wisely

*Our senior leaders are expected to have moved around the firm, reinventing knowledge and building new relationships. They go through cycles of experience and we encourage them to move every three to five years: either to overseas or to different locations, teams or cultures to experience a different background and to immerse themselves in a different world. They must be willing to take risks and try different paths.*

LAURA HINTON, CHIEF PEOPLE OFFICER, PWC LLP UK

## Breadth of experience as an accelerator

As we saw in Chapter 2, breadth of experience is the foundation for accelerating a high-potential employee's career. It is a prerequisite for moving to more senior roles. Only if a promising employee has worked through a range of different organizational challenges will they be able to deal effectively with the scale and complexity of a leadership role, may that be as the head of finance or HR, or as a general manager.

Being exposed to different experiences allows a leader to develop a broader perspective and better cross-organizational business understanding, which will serve as an important foundation for better decision-making. Furthermore, breadth of experience makes high-potential employees more flexible, both in terms of how they approach their careers and how they tackle job-related challenges; moving between roles provides many new impulses as well as exposure to new processes and ways of doing things. This means that a high-potential employee is forced to learn how to adapt their leadership style to remain effective. In addition, breadth of experience encourages a person to try new roles. Once a high-potential employee has learned that they have the necessary transferable skills to add value in a new business area, they are more likely to leave their comfort zone and try new roles again in future.

Finally, breadth fosters innovation. High-potential employees are more likely to find creative solutions if they have been forced to deviate from their tried and tested methods in the past and if they have witnessed different ways of solving problems in other business units or countries.

While breadth has always been an important foundation for a business leader's success, it has become even more of a prerequisite given the disruptions and fast technological changes that we explored in Chapter 1. Breadth of experience is now also important for traditionally more focused career paths such as the head of functions (eg legal, HR or marketing). Functional and technical leaders also need exposure to roles outside their area of functional expertise to better equip themselves for the changes that digitalization, emerging markets and other technological changes are creating.

Even if a high-potential employee does not want to become a leader, breadth of experience will serve them well in a business environment where digital disruption, artificial intelligence and many other technological advances continually challenge the status quo. Simply wanting to stay in their job means having to learn how to adapt. If a high-potential employee is not prepared to grow with their job, the job will eventually outgrow them.

To accelerate leaders, we must therefore provide access to a variety of different roles that provide an emerging leader with a variety of experiences. We must consider carefully which blank spaces on the person's CV a role will help to fill. We must also ensure that no time is unnecessarily wasted by 'treading water' when a high-potential employee has stopped learning and is no longer challenged. Not only do we risk slowing down an emerging leader's progression, we may also increase the risk of them becoming disengaged and subsequently leaving our organization in search of a new challenge.

## Critical job assignments

Various frameworks have been suggested that set out the experiences, or critical job assignments, that leaders need to get exposure to and master as they progress to the top of an organization. There is general agreement among these frameworks, including my own 9 Critical Job Assignments Framework, that formative roles and projects include the experiences set out in Figure 3.1.[1, 2, 3, 4]

Interestingly, many organizations do not have official frameworks or definitions of the types of experiences they expect their rising stars to gain on their way to leadership roles. But even where organizations do not have any frameworks in place, most interviewees were able to set out the types of experiences that a successful leader requires as part of their leadership development journey. As we will see throughout this chapter, these roles mirror the experiences listed in Figure 3.1.

The In Practice box below shows different examples of the roles and experiences that leaders in different functions and different industry sectors are expected to pass through. While some interviewees have argued that the types of experiences that are important for an emerging leader are driven by the role the leader is aiming for or by the part of the organization they are in or the business cycle the organization currently finds itself in (growth versus contraction), comparing the examples shared by HR leaders across many different industry sectors, there was little noticeable difference in the experiences they listed as being important. This is probably not surprising as the roles that help leaders develop should prepare these emerging leaders to work successfully in any part of an organization and across any phase of an organization's life cycle, be it growth, restructure or turnaround.

**Figure 3.1** Formative leadership experiences

## In practice: breadth as an accelerator across industry sectors

### General manager in the apparel industry

Our unofficial list of experiences for general managerial roles includes practical experience in the sales and marketing area, and of course the experience of managing people. You should have worked abroad, and ideally you should also have experience of working in at least one headquarters' function such as legal, HR, finance or supply chain.

Matthias Kempf, former Vice President
Human Resources Emerging Markets, adidas Group

### General manager in the steel industry

For operational roles, people whom we promote into senior roles tend all to be industrial people. They have run big plants and have deep industry knowledge. They have managed a large number of people. They are resilient, strong characters and have broad leadership; some have only ever worked in Europe. Generally, to succeed in this organization, resilience is important and so are deep business and finance experience. We will explore different rotations across the business. What rotation a person needs will depend on their profile. Maybe they transfer functions from HR to sales. We decide this on an individual basis. If you have a person with a well-rounded profile, they are going to be a well-rounded leader.

Brian Callaghan, Global Head of Leadership Development,
Executive Resourcing & Corporate University,
Global Steel & Mining Organization

### Senior leaders in the automotive industry

We have three main criteria. International experience is important. You should have spent at least two years abroad. You also need cross-functional moves, for example from engineering to R&D or from automotive to one of the corporate functions. And you need a cross-organizational move.

Matthias Metzger, Global Head of Talent Management &
Organizational Development, Continental AG

## Senior leaders in the retail industry

The most critical time is the manager of managers or head of department level. People need seven to ten years' experience to get to this level. Once at this level, they need to go through three critical and different experiences. As a general manager you need experience in operations, product, customer and marketing. At the head of department level, we give people boundary-spanning moves. We need to give them breadth for future moves. These moves really prepare you for the top roles. They manage a unit, budget and large teams. These are the most senior operational roles. It gives them breadth and oversight. You either work in a small, large or international store, you do a turnaround store or you do a brand new store. But you don't do three brand new stores in a row. Boundary-spanning moves are moves that take you up one level, they take you to different countries or to a very different experience. These are really uncomfortable moves as they expose people to something very new. You don't get learning and stretch with familiar situations.

HR Leader, Global Organization

## The headhunter's perspective

Although you need to be able to hold your own technically, you don't need deep knowledge. I have never told anyone, 'you need more technical experience'. Raw IQ helps you pick up new things quickly. And you need the people piece which relates to emotional intelligence. Characteristics for accelerated learning include exposure to a significantly different environment, an agile mindset, taking risks and working with senior executives. Sometimes I find that people lack important experience. For example, they cannot break out of a programme director role in IT and they really need to get more exposure to sales. This doesn't mean that they need to go into a sales role. They could work with the sales team in a support role instead. They just need to get closer to the customer. The other scenario is the need for more financial exposure. You need to get a number, whatever it is, even just a budget to manage. It's important to show that you can balance the books or ensure that an account is profitable. It's difficult to move from a technical role to a front-line/P&L role at senior level.

Mary Lawrance, Founder, Cariance Executive Search & Consulting

The only consideration for what type of stretch role an emerging leader should take up as part of their development should be the person's development needs. The more thorough the assessment of these development needs is, the more powerful the choice of stretch assignment for the person will be. Development needs can be assessed effectively through performance reviews, 360-degree feedback, psychometric profiling or assessment centres. We will further delve into the role of assessments and candidate profiling, important elements of successful acceleration, in Chapter 6. Another reason for focusing simply on experiences, rather than the specific role that an emerging leader is ultimately aiming for, is the danger that jobs and career paths can become outdated very quickly in the wake of ongoing organizational restructures and industry volatility.

Let's look at the most frequently mentioned experiences that emerging leaders benefit from in preparation for moving to senior management role. For each experience, I will explore the challenges associated with the experience as well as the learning and fine-tuning of leadership capabilities that the leader can expect to take away from the experience. I explored each of these roles in detail in my last book *Where Have All the Senior Women Gone? 9 Critical Job Assignments for Women Leaders.*[5]

## Working internationally

In Europe, we have a multicultural organization that sometimes is difficult to manage, as collaboration across the teams is not so easy. So we have created a mobility programme to allow our high-potentials to experience different realities and develop their resilience and adaptation capacities. Being abroad and experiencing different contexts helps to improve collaboration.

Susana Simões, Regional Lead EMEA, Learning & Development,
Global Electronics Organization

Even when organizations have not specified any critical job assignments and where interviewees were not able to specify in detail the types of experiences that the organization values, the one critical job assignment that was mentioned by most HR leaders was international experience. Given the international nature of most large organizations this is not surprising. International experience is also one of the experiences that takes an emerging leader out of their comfort zone more than any other roles. Managers often take up offers of international assignment expecting significant career development.[6,7] Working internationally can take two forms. First, the classic international assignment or overseas posting where the emerging leader lives and works abroad for a few months or even years. Or alternatively, global roles, where they remain in their home country and work with one or more international regions. Frequent travel is often a requirement of global roles, as is virtual working where a high-potential employee has to manage a team remotely. Virtual working comes with its own challenges such as building trust, cohesion, effective communication and performance management at a distance.[8] At home, the emerging leader's working life tends to be safe and supported by a trusted network of colleagues, friends and family. They probably have a clear understanding of what is expected of them and have an established track record of successful job performance. Once abroad, everything changes. The new role brings with it new markets, customers and working practices. And it doesn't stop there. To start with, the emerging leader doesn't have a personal support network and will be an outsider whose value to the new team has yet to be proven.

The challenges posed by working internationally are clearly significant but so is the learning gained from this experience.[9] To succeed, emerging leaders must start with a clear definition of their role and a good understanding of the organization's expectations of what they will achieve. Next, it's time to build relationships and establish credibility with local teams, customers and suppliers. To do this effectively, they must listen actively and learn from others by respecting their points of view, which may be different from their own. This will help the high-potential employee to develop a good understanding of the local market and its customers and increase their understanding of international business. Above all, they must be prepared to leave their comfort zone by fully opening up to the new culture. This includes adopting local customs and ways of doing business, as well as trying their hand at speaking the local language. All this will help the emerging leader to deliver results globally.

Living and working abroad is no small feat, particularly at the beginning when everything is new. Perseverance and resilience are key attributes to making international assignments a success. Working globally is a highly effective time for personal development as we continuously uncover our own assumptions and biases about who we are and how the world works. The subsequent questioning and realignment of strongly held beliefs creates effective development. It is this critical questioning of taken-for-granted assumptions that allows for effective learning. We will come back to the topic of perspective transformation and reflective learning in Chapter 7. It is difficult, if not impossible, to achieve this type of personal development back home.

While international assignments are the most commonly named leadership experience and are hard to match in terms of the learning they offer, they are also among the most difficult to execute successfully. Many expatriate managers leave their assignments early. Many also leave their employers within 12 to 18 months of having returned from an assignment even if it was successful.[10] This is often because organizations are either not recognizing the newly gained skills of the former expat or because they are not able to offer the high-potential employee a more senior role. Organizations can and should support emerging leaders on an international assignment, including offering regular readiness conversations to ensure everyone, and not only the most mobile, have access to this learning experience; also practical help with relocation (schools, housing, language and etiquette training), mentors back at home to stay in touch and a clear return policy to ensure that expat managers find stretching roles on their return.

## Managing change

Change is a constant for most organizations. Not much time passes between significant realignment of processes, culture or overall business strategy. In a fast-moving world, organizations must stay agile and respond to both internal and external needs. At its most basic, being capable of working effectively through the upheaval of organizational change, of continuing to deliver results and staying engaged, is a vital ability of high-potential employees. For those who are hoping to take on leadership roles, being able to implement change or even driving change, often at an organizational level, is vital. High-potential employees must learn to stay effective themselves and not become personally absorbed in their own concerns about the impending changes. The two main challenges that allow a high-potential employee to hone their leadership skills in change projects are dealing with uncertainty as well as dealing with people's emotions, both of which are frequently caused by the disruption that organizational change brings.[11] Throughout the change process there is likely to be a lack of clarity and information about how new processes and ways of working will impact the employee's roles. As an effective change agent, emerging leaders must develop the ability to make decisions based on the best available information rather than waiting for more information to become available. Furthermore, they must learn how to help allay their own and others' fears in these situations. Change can create fear of the unknown, of a potential loss of our power base or rewards, and concerns that our current skills may either no longer be valued or that they may no longer be sufficient to deal effectively with new roles.

Proactive and frequent communication, even when there is nothing new to communicate, and messages that appeal at both an emotional and a rational level, are crucial to help others deal with the upheaval of change.[12] The ability to move processes and people from the status quo to a new way of working is an important experience to gain.

## Creating something from scratch

Start-up experience is helpful as it allows you to develop so many of the other things that are crucial: change management, getting others to follow you. It is about painting a picture of the future.

Dr Siobhan Martin, Executive Director UK HR, Mercer

Innovation and renewal are important for organizations. Without it, organizations are rarely able to survive in today's fast-moving, competitive world. Corporate entrepreneurship is commonly referred to as *intrapreneurship* and refers to creating something new that has not existed before. This could be a new system or process, a new service or product, or even a new business line. Importantly, intrapreneurship includes both a viable business idea as well as the successful execution of this idea. It's not only about brilliant ideas.[13, 14]

While large organizations often have the resources necessary for a new venture, the emerging leader must nevertheless put forward a strong case as to why these resources ought to be made available for their venture instead of another project. New business-within-a-business ventures are also far from risk-free. In most cases, there is no guarantee that the new venture will be successful and create the revenue or competitive advantage that is forecast. As a result, the high-potential employee is taking a potential risk to their reputation in the company. The intrapreneur must overcome several hurdles, which provide great leadership development opportunities. Building something new requires a vision as well as a detailed business plan of what the new function, product or process will look like and, more importantly, what it will do for the organization. An intrapreneur's business plan must cover everything from cash flow projections and marketing propositions to staffing plans and operational considerations. Support for the new business idea must be garnered across the organization. Supporters come in many different shapes and forms. Senior supporters are particularly important as they will act as advocates and defenders of the idea; they also help to secure resources. A new idea, the request for scarce organizational resources, no guarantee that the new venture will work – without the intrapreneur's personal credibility, no new business venture will get very far. Responses such as 'This cannot be done' and 'The organization is not set up to realize this vision' are not uncommon. Counter to popular perceptions, large organizations tend to generate a lot of ideas but often fail at the implementation stage due to bureaucracy and infrastructure constraints.[15]

While intrapreneurs may have to do a lot of the work themselves, depending on the scope of the project, they may also need a team. It is important to find people who are willing to work on a venture where success is not guaranteed. Furthermore, they must learn to adapt their leadership style to different challenges throughout the start-up project: giving clear direction in times of uncertainty, instilling belief in the cause, and making decisions when little data is available. Once all the challenges are overcome, start-up projects provide a powerful and visible legacy for the high-potential employee.

## Creating growth

The very essence of an organization is to grow, to increase revenue and profitability. Growth is a key factor when investors value organizations and while it is often high-growth technology organizations that take the limelight, large established companies are also measured on their growth, even if theirs is a steadier rate of growth. Growth is typically achieved through two different routes: investment in new assets or improving the efficiency of existing assets. Innovation can also play a role, where radically new ideas create customer growth or open new market spaces by creating products or services for which there are no direct competitors. Growth generates excitement and it's often an all-hands-to-the pump scenario as growth outstrips existing capacity; it is also a time that generates new development opportunities for the emerging leader.

While growth in high-growth companies may be a matter of dealing with exceptional external demand, creating growth in more established organizations may require a more deliberate strategy. The high-potential employee needs to identify the best chances for winning customers, develop an understanding of the best channels to market and customer acquisition. With this comes a commitment to growth and a need to set specific and challenging goals. To achieve these, the emerging leader must negotiate access to organizational resources to support their growth targets and actively use their contacts in the organization. The high-potential employee's external networks will also come in helpful when delivering against these targets. The emerging leader must know their customers well and stay close to them, particularly if the desired growth is driven by new product development and innovation.

Creating growth is a balancing act between focusing on numbers and commercial opportunities on the one hand and people on the other. The people to focus on include both customers and those around the emerging leader who will help them deliver value for customers. In short, numbers need to add up and people need to be brought into the vision.

## Fixing problems

Turnaround experts are the fire-fighters of the corporate world. When products fail, when customers are deeply unhappy and profits start to plummet, they come to the rescue. While all projects must be executed at pace, turnaround projects are a step up from more orderly organizational change programmes. They require immediate, and at times drastic, action.[16]

A high-potential employee is unlikely to be entrusted with large-scale turnaround projects until some way into their career, as these projects require strong change management and leadership skills, alongside a good dose of resilience. However, early exposure to smaller turnaround projects, such as taking on the account management of the most dissatisfied customer in the team or getting involved in a product recall provide important leadership experiences.

Things go wrong all the time and being able to demonstrate that an emerging leader is good at fixing problems effectively without losing their cool under pressure is a skill that marks them out as leaders. As part of a turnaround project, they need to fix three problems: the immediate crisis, people issues and, finally, processes. First up, they need to identify the root cause of the problem without getting side-tracked by too much analysis. They then need to act quickly to stabilize the situation. This requires judgement and fast decision-making. Once the immediate crisis has been averted, it is time to focus on re-establishing commitment and re-energizing people. The high-potential employee must develop a vision of the way forward, create excitement and gain buy-in. Crisis situations can make this more challenging as they often represent a broken environment where people have become suspicious and are no longer cooperating. Strong communication and influencing skills are necessary but often not enough to get the message across – emerging leaders also need to show empathy and be good listeners. Finally, they must focus on putting in place new processes. After the situation has been stabilized and adrenaline levels have dropped, it is tempting to move on to a new challenge. However, processes and metrics are required to ensure that the necessary improvements are delivered. Without these, it is all too easy to slip back into old ways of doing things.

## Working in a different environment

It is tempting to stay in a familiar environment. The function where we learned our profession is well known to us. We understand its culture and know how to get things done – we are experts. However, only if we move outside our comfort zone is our thinking challenged and we are forced to learn new ways of solving problems and delivering results.

Moving to a different role does not mean a promotion to a somewhat more senior version of the job that we have been doing; it involves a real step change, such as moving to a different function or business unit. Cross-functional moves, particularly those from areas such as HR, legal or finance to an operational area, such as a call centre or a manufacturing plant, become increasingly difficult as we become more senior and are therefore best tackled early on.

Moving to a different environment brings several challenges as the high-potential employee finds themselves on 'alien turf' and must adapt to a new working culture and new stakeholders. However, their new surroundings will increase the emerging leader's business understanding and force them to adapt their way of working, which will make them more flexible, an important leadership attribute. The emerging leader also needs to learn fast to make an impact and deliver quick wins. These early results are vital if they are to establish credibility with experts in the new area who may be sceptical about the value they can add.

Often, no training and little support are provided in the new role. Realizing that they don't know *what* they need to know and *who* they need to know is one of the most painful discoveries during a stretch assignment. Building new relationships, listening and asking questions increases the emerging leader's capacity to find new ways of being effective again.

Frequently, the most important take-away lesson from working in a different environment is the confidence that our transferable skills allow us to add value without having to rely on technical knowledge. This enables us to demonstrate that past achievements can be replicated in unfamiliar territory, which is a much sought-after quality in fast-moving organizations that constantly come up against new challenges.

## Managing people

Operational experience is a key stepping stone on the career ladder in most organizations. It provides us with a vital understanding of the day-to-day running of a business. In these roles, we are responsible for operating and improving the systems that produce and deliver an organization's products or services, such as manufacturing, supply chain management or call centre operations. What roles are classed as operational roles depends on what products a company is producing or what services it is offering. Operational roles in an organization that produces physical goods, such as a fast-moving goods company or a car manufacturer, may involve working in plants where the high-potential employee is responsible for machinery, meeting production goals and health and safety. Operational roles in service-based organizations, such as a telecommunications organization or a bank, may involve managing aspects of customer service, for example running a call centre, client support centre or processing centre. In these situations, an operational role allows a high-potential employee to learn about delivering results for a customer end to end.

Operational roles are always at the core of what a company delivers as opposed to functional roles that provide important support services, such as human resources, legal and finance. As the emerging leader gains more operational experience, they increasingly gain responsibility for entire parts of a business. This may involve being responsible for larger teams, multiple operational sites and working in a more complex matrix set-up. It may also involve elements of profit and loss accountability.

True profit and loss accountability is only held by a small number of people at senior level who are responsible for both profit centres, for example sales in certain geographical regions, as well as cost centres, such as production, marketing and HR. At a less senior level, operational experience often means working in a very clearly output-focused environment where operations or sales numbers are reported on a quarterly or monthly basis. This numbers-driven way of working provides an acute understanding of costs, margins and efficiencies, and with it a clear understanding of the core drivers of business. At the same time, these numbers provide a clear indication of the emerging leader's personal performance.

The high-potential employee must be clear about their targets. Establishing channels and processes to ensure clear and ongoing communication as well as balancing a focus on processes, people and budgets are key ingredients to ensuring successful delivery. They must also monitor outputs to ensure high-quality standards and delivery to time and budget, and address underperformance swiftly by addressing process shortcomings and improving people skills. With everyday delivery secured, it also pays to identify opportunities for further improvements, which must then be implemented and evaluated for effectiveness.

The high-potential employee can show that they are good at getting things done and that they can deliver results. But there are of course times when targets are not achieved, which will be highly visible. It requires grit to get through these times. Furthermore, operational experience allows the high-potential employee to make decisions based on an understanding of core business drivers. Senior leaders respect this understanding and as a result, high-potential employees gain in credibility. The emerging leader is no longer seen as a functional expert but as having highly valuable insights into how the core of the organization works, a crucial leadership experience. It pays to try out operational roles early on. The more senior and the more technically specialist an emerging leader becomes, the more difficult it becomes to move to operational roles.

## People management

Organizations are social systems that bring together different people to work towards realizing an organization's vision. Being able to harness the energies of other people and getting everyone working towards the same goal is vital to delivering outstanding results.

People management is a good experience to start developing early, even if initially only on an informal basis, such as managing interns or being a mentor to a new colleague. Taking on formal management responsibility for a small team represents an important transition from being an individual contributor to achieving results through others.[17] With increasing levels of seniority, people management frequently moves from managing smaller groups of people in relatively stable environments, to managing larger groups of people through challenges such as organizational change and crises.

The transition from an individual contributor to a team manager can have its challenges. The emerging leader has yet to learn to stop doing their former job and instead start delivering through others. If they continue to do what they used to be good at, they will frustrate their team through micro-management. A strong team can deal with day-to-day problems and provide the high-potential employee with the headroom to focus on bigger-picture issues and forward planning.[18]

Building a strong team involves several skills, such as creating a shared vision and joint meaning, understanding individuals' strengths and weaknesses and creating a team environment where everyone works together well. This requires a combination of influencing and good listening, as well as showing a genuine interest in others. It also means being clear about what is expected, delegating work and monitoring progress. Furthermore, the emerging leader must support the team through training and coaching, and at times address people problems and underperformance. They must resist the temptation to hope that these issues will resolve themselves and instead address them with decisiveness and tact. Finally, they need to be flexible in their leadership style and recognize that their team's approach to work may be different to their own. These skills allow the emerging leader to build an environment in which others can work to their full potential. As a result, the emerging leader can deliver outstanding results time and again.

## Technical skills

Technical skills tend not to be the focus of critical job assignments for leadership development. Developmental stretch assignments tend to focus on transferable leadership skills. However, a role where an emerging leader must get to grips with a lot of new technical knowledge at great depth may be classed as a critical job assignment. In this situation, it is learning how to acquire this new knowledge quickly and staying up to date, as well as applying the knowledge, that constitutes the development and not the knowledge itself.

A number of technical skills were mentioned by the interviewees as important ingredients for accelerated leadership development. These skills reflect business priority areas, such as risk management, digital skills, as well as a broader set of fundamental business skills, for example financial acumen, project management and business acumen. It can be argued that these are highly transferable skills that will benefit any leader in addition to honing their leadership behaviours.

## Summary

Stretch assignments are one of the most powerful ways to acquire new knowledge and hone existing capabilities. While some elements of leadership qualities can be taught on courses, it is only through real-life application that we can make sense of this learning and become expert at applying it.

When it comes to developing leaders, some experiences seem to be more developmental than others as they provide certain challenges that lend themselves to gaining and fine-tuning leadership capabilities. These experiences range from delivering results at the core of an organization, such as operational delivery, to growing something or starting something from scratch, changing existing processes and cultures to radical turnaround. Working in a different environment or abroad are two other formative experiences as they often challenge commonly held beliefs. People management and a core of technical skills are also part of the leadership development journey. These experiences will allow a leader to hone the leadership capabilities that are required for success in the VUCA world: learning agility, flexibility in leadership style and the readiness to question one's assumptions; innovation, influencing and business-wide perspectives for decision-making in a volatile business world.

Not every leader will go through every single one of these experiences and their ordering may vary. However, every leader is likely to go through a significant number of these experiences on the way to the top as part of filling blank spaces on their CV. It is important to define experiences and not roles when deciding what critical job assignment a high-potential employee will move into.

In the next chapter, we will look at how organizations give high-potential employees access to these types of experiences. As we will see, this can range from formal rotation programmes to informal, temporary assignments and projects that are taken on in addition to the emerging leader's day job.

## Organizational design tips

- **Focus on experiences rather than roles and career paths.** Clearly define the types of experiences that you expect your leaders to have gained rather than spending resources on developing detailed career maps, which can quickly become outdated as organizations undergo significant change and restructuring.

- **Regular readiness assessments.** Build readiness assessments for more logistically challenging assignments, such as international assignments or operational roles, into half-yearly or yearly development conversations to ensure that everyone has access to these roles. If a high-potential employee cannot take up an opportunity now, they may be able to do so the following year.

- **Provide support for international assignments.** This should include practical help with relocation (schools, housing, language and etiquette training), mentors back at home to stay in touch, and a clear return policy to ensure that expat managers find stretching roles once back home.

- **Timing.** Help high-potential employees understand that some assignments may be easier to do early on in a career, for example operational delivery and international assignments. Ensure that your HR processes are aligned to make it easier for people to move across organizations.

## Individual coaching tips

- **Look for breadth of experience.** Take some time to assess your experiences to date to identify what you have had plenty of exposure to and what you are missing. Once you have identified your experience gaps, develop a plan for how to get exposure to people, projects or roles that will help you gain the missing experience. It does not have to be a six-month placement or a full-time role. Try shadowing people, adding additional stretch to your current role or volunteering your time for a developmental project outside of work.

- **Start early and be mindful of the developmental value of each experience.** If you want to move fast, breadth of experience that allows you to cover blank spaces on your CV will help you to do so. Be mindful about what new skills you can learn in new projects or roles. The earlier you start, the earlier you can demonstrate your capability to take on new roles and make them a success. This in turn will open doors to new roles.

- **Start your readiness assessment early.** Make sure you get all those impacted by your potential job move on side early and demonstrate that you are ready for the move. This may include moving within the country, changing the hours you work, more frequent travel, or even moving abroad for a period of time.

- **Look for stretch projects in addition to your main job.** In addition to your main role look for further opportunities to gain initial exposure to some of the leadership experiences explored in this chapter. This will allow you to make the right contacts and help to secure a full-time role later. Developing outside of work by getting involved in a charity or not-for-profit organization is another way to gain additional experience. It doesn't always have to be a full-time role.

- **Identify the right people.** If you are looking for a particular development opportunity, identify people in your organization who are known for these types of roles. They will be able to help you understand what exactly is required for these roles and may consider you for a role on one of their next projects or know of other people who are looking for new team members.

# Notes

**1** Wichert, I (2011) *Where Have All the Senior Women Gone? 9 critical job assignments for women leaders*, Palgrave Macmillan, Basingstoke

**2** McCall, MW, Lombardo, MM and Morrison, AM (1988) *Lessons of Experience: How successful executives develop on the job*, The Free Press, New York

**3** Dotlich, DL, Noel, JL and Walker, N (2004) *Leadership Passages: The personal and professional transitions that make or break a leader*, Jossey-Bass, San Francisco, CA

**4** McCauley, CD (1999) *Learning from Work Experience: The job challenges profile*, Jossey-Bass/Pfeiffer, San Francisco, CA

**5** Wichert, I (2011) *Where Have All the Senior Women Gone? 9 critical job assignments for women leaders*, Palgrave Macmillan, Basingstoke

**6** Dickman, M, Doherty, N, Mills, T and Brewster, C (2008) Why do they go? Individual and corporate perspectives on the factors influencing the decision to accept an international assignment, *The International Journal of Human Resources Management*, **19** (4), pp 731–51

**7** Dickman, M and Doherty, N (2008) Exploring the career capital impact of international assignments within distinct organisational contexts, *British Journal of Management*, **19**, pp 145–61

**8** Kirkman, BL, Rosen, B, Gibson, CB, Tesluk, PE and McPherson, SO (2002) Five challenges to virtual team success: Lessons from Sabre, Inc, *Academy of Management Perspectives*, **16**, pp 67–79

**9** Moon, JA (2004) *A Handbook for Reflective and Experiential Learning: Theory and practice*, Routledge, Abingdon

**10** Wilson, MS and Dalton, MA (1998) *International Success: Selecting, developing and supporting expatriate managers*, Center for Creative Leadership, Greenboro, NC

**11** By, RT (2005) Organisational change management: A critical review, *Journal of Change Management*, **5** (4), 369–80

**12** Elvin, WJL (2005) The role of communication in organisational change, *Corporate Communications: An International Journal*, **10**, pp 129–38

**13** Pinchot, G (1985) *Intrapreneuring: Why you don't have to leave your organization to become an entrepreneur*, Harper & Row, New York

**14** Thornberry, NE (2003) Corporate entrepreneurship: Teaching managers to be entrepreneurs, *Journal of Management Development*, 4, 329–44

**15** Pinchot, G (1985) *Intrapreneuring: Why you don't have to leave your organization to become an entrepreneur*, Harper & Row, New York

**16** Slatter, S, Lovett, D and Barlow, L (2006) *Leading Corporate Turnaround: How leaders fix troubled companies*, John Wiley, Chichester, UK

**17** Charan, R, Drotter, S and Noel, J (2001) *The Leadership Pipeline: How to build the leadership-empowered company*, Jossey-Bass, San Francisco, CA

**18** Charan, R, Drotter, S and Noel, J (2001) *The Leadership Pipeline: How to build the leadership-empowered company*, Jossey-Bass, San Francisco, CA

# Learning on the job

04

## Organizational development approaches

*Our talent on the accelerated programme moves faster in their personal career than those who don't attend the programme. But we need even more acceleration to develop more breadth as people move to top management. Employees who start with rotations early have a different and much more versatile perspective. They also develop a better network and the ability to approach issues from a holistic point of view.*

URSULA SCHWARZENBART, HEAD OF TALENT DEVELOPMENT & DIVERSITY MANAGEMENT, DAIMLER AG

*We do placements early on to build cross-functional experience. People are strongly encouraged to collaborate and knowledge share, where it brings value. We are a complex organization regarding our structure and products. While this breeds diversity, it makes it harder to collaborate. Experiential learning gets people into projects where they can be autonomous and where they can make mistakes. We need to be able to deal with failure. We need an openness to risk-taking.*

SELINA MILLSTAM, VICE PRESIDENT & GLOBAL HEAD OF TALENT MANAGEMENT, ERICSSON

## Introduction

In this chapter we will continue to explore the timing and format of the different leadership experiences that we examined in the last chapter, such as start-up and turnaround experience.

On-the-job learning, also known as experiential learning, is an important part of leadership development. From a certain stage onward, the learning that emerging leaders require is no longer able to be transferred on training courses. Instead, emerging leaders must hone their leadership capability by experiencing novel and increasingly complex situations. Experiential learning involves an ongoing transaction between the high-potential employee and their environment. According to David Kolb in his seminal work on experiential learning, experience continually reshapes the high-potential employees' ideas and concepts of the world and allows them to acquire and test knowledge.[1]

David Kolb goes on to state that, 'Learning is the process whereby knowledge is created through the transformation of experience' (p 38). While not a scientifically precise figure, Lombardo and Eichinger have suggested a 70:20:10 model, which indicates that experiential learning accounts for about 70 per cent of development.[2] A further 20 per cent of development comes from learning through others, such as mentors and sponsors, and a mere 10 per cent is contributed by classroom-based learning. Classroom-based learning helps us learn the theories, principles and tools of a skill or topic, but it is only through the practical application of this newly acquired knowledge that we can fully make sense of it. Another way to test and consolidate our knowledge is through other people, the 20 per cent referred to in Lombardo and Eichinger's model. Others can act as role models and allow us to observe how they apply the principles and tools we have learned about in the classroom. Furthermore, they can give us helpful feedback about our own application of these theories and principles.

For experiential learning to be effective, the high-potential employee must pass through four stages of the learning process:[3, 4]

- **Exposure to a concrete experience** and the readiness to fully open themselves up to the experience. This is the *feeling* part of an experience.

- **Reflective observation**, which involves describing, questioning and interpreting an experience and making sense of it. It is a prerequisite of the next two stages and represents the *watching* part of the experience.

- **Abstract conceptualization** where the high-potential employee must abstract a specific experience and integrate it with existing theories and views of the world. This integration allows the high-potential employee to bring together a wide range of seemingly unconnected experiences and integrate them into theories. This allows them to generalize their new learning and apply it to future situations. It represents the *thinking* part of the experience.

- **Active experimentation** focuses on amending existing theories, knowledge or views of the world. It focuses on how the high-potential employee will approach future situations differently. It refers to the *doing* part of the experience.

This is not a sequential, one-time process. Kolb points to the importance of the high-potential employee toggling between the two extremes of concrete experience on the one hand and abstract conceptualization on the other. Furthermore, he points to the importance of being able to move between both reflective observation and active experimentation. The high-potential employee must be able to move across all four stages, back and forth, if they are to extract maximum learning from an experience. We will delve into the role of reflective learning, the second step in Kolb's model, and examine how organizations can encourage this important activity in more detail in Chapter 7.

On-the-job learning is not only an effective way of acquiring, testing and fine-tuning important leadership skills and knowledge; it is also a more cost-effective solution to classroom learning, especially if it is up to the individual to find their own stretch assignments rather than relying on an organizational infrastructure to secure these roles. It also reflects the self-sufficiency ethos that most organizations subscribe to in relation to career development. As we saw in Chapter 2, organizations expect their employees to drive their own development and to take charge of their careers. Only a small number of carefully selected, high-potential talent or critical talent groups, such as early-career talent or future leadership talent, are placed on formal accelerated leadership development programmes with a more structured offer of development and career management support.

Before we look at the types of programmes that may be most effective at giving emerging leaders access to the experiences that we explored in the last chapter, such as people-management or operational delivery experience, let's look at timing first. At what career stage or age is it most effective to actively build breadth into an emerging leader's career? Can this be done at any point or are some points more conducive to effective broadening out than others?

## When is breadth important?

While a small number of the HR leaders interviewed insist that an employee's experience base can be developed and broadened out at any age and at any stage of their career, there generally seem to be two points that are most effective for developing breadth: early on in a person's career, sometimes as early as the graduate programme; and second, as people are getting ready to move to senior management. Both of these career stages have different advantages and disadvantages for broadening out a high-potential employee's experience base.

If we introduce breadth and job rotation early in an employee's career, they are likely to develop an organization-wide perspective, a 'can-do' attitude and a powerful network that will keep propelling their career in the future. Furthermore, the early experience of taking on new challenges and giving things 'a go' shapes an employee's attitude positively towards future risk-taking and leaving their comfort zone.

However, the challenge with injecting breadth early in a high-potential's career is working out what experiences lend themselves best to this early acceleration and identifying high-quality projects or assignments for an individual. Furthermore, this early experience is likely to be at a level where an emerging leader may not yet be able to practise making important business decisions, leading large teams or managing significant parts of the business. Early breadth may therefore have to be topped up with another round of broadening out at a more senior level.

The advantage of broadening out at middle management, in preparation for moving to senior roles, is that high-potential employees have already gathered significant work experience. They are no longer novices and have learned to operate effectively in an organization. Stretch roles at this level can therefore provide the emerging leader with the opportunity to take on roles with significant decision-making power and responsibility.

For middle-management acceleration, there is, however, the temptation to progress high-potentials upwards rather than giving them the dwell time and the opportunity to take two or three very different roles at the same level to build the breadth that will equip them for the final push to senior management. We will explore the importance of dwell time as a success factor for acceleration in the next chapter.

Let's look at both graduate and senior management development programmes in turn.

## Graduate programmes

Organizations run a variety of programmes to explicitly accelerate their high-potential talent early on in their career. As we can see in the examples in the In Practice box below and in Table 4.1, these programmes share several features.

The vision is always to accelerate young talent and to build the foundation for a future leadership talent pool. In some cases, organizations even define what level they expect participants to have reached once they have completed the programme. In most cases, this is manager level.

Although not always explicitly stated, these programmes tend to use a 70:20:10 approach, where exposure to a series of stretch roles is supported by mentors, and further supplemented with formal training. Not all programmes include all three elements and instead adopt a blended approach that incorporates two of these three elements.

While many of the programmes are focused on graduates straight out of university, some are focused on early-career incumbents or even more broadly, millennials. Several organizations offer an accelerated programme alongside their standard graduate programme. Graduates or early-career professionals who either did particularly well during the initial assessment or who stood out in the early days of the graduate programme are sometimes selected into a smaller, more advanced programme with a focus on acceleration and additional support.

Most of the graduate programmes use six- or nine-month rotations across roles and countries to expose high-potential employees to various parts of the organization. These programmes tend to run for a total of between 18 months and 2 years.

Psychometric testing seems to feature in almost all programmes as part of the selection process. And the more stretching the programme is, the more stringent the selection process. In some cases, for example where the programme includes a higher number of job rotations in a short period of time or where participants are supposed to reach a certain management level by the end of the programme, the selection process often includes extensive psychometric profiling as well as an assessment centre.

### In practice: programmes to accelerate at early-career level

We have a graduate programme for 9 to 12 months where we select about 20 to 30. From there we select two or three candidates for our Elevator Programme. We put these candidates through the wringer: verbal and numerical reasoning tests and personality assessments. It's an 18-month programme with exposure to all key disciplines, such as commercial, HR and finance. They have project work in two different countries which are not their home country and at two different properties. Often the language is foreign. In total, they do two 9-month placements. They are learning about different elements of the business. When they are finished with the programme, they are close to a manager role, for example outlet manager role in busy property. Then they are tested in role and we keep an eye on them and keep fast-tracking their career.

Brendan Toomey, Vice President, Human Resources
Asia Pacific, Hilton

We have a Rockstar Programme where people go through an application and interview process. It is an accelerated 10-month programme with 10 modules. What worked really well was when we gave these young people a real problem to solve. As a senior site management team, we were good at developing site strategy but then we always ran out of time implementing these ideas. We started giving the Rockstar participants these projects to complete and it has worked extremely well. These young people liked having an impact. For one programme targeted at a specific LOB [line of business] we achieved a 12 to 30 per cent market share increase as we had additional hands and legs to get projects completed. And the young people could say: 'I helped this business grow'.

Stephen Caulfield, Vice President Global Field Services & GM Dell Bratislava, Dell EMC Global Services

We have acceleration programmes for graduates, young professionals and special target groups. Typically, the programmes consist of different modules (actual and virtual) and participants get specific tasks that are completed through action learning. At the end of the programme, the teams present the results back to our senior leadership team. This provides visibility. Participants get a mentor and a sponsor and build their network.

Matthias Metzger, Global Head of Talent Management & Organizational Development, Continental AG

All the HR and business leaders interviewed agreed that successful participants showed several impressive characteristics at the end of the acceleration programme including:

- can-do attitude;
- collaboration;
- openness to trying new things;
- readiness to take calculated risks and the ability to deal with failure;
- organization-wide perspective;
- extended network;
- faster progression.

Despite their advantages, acceleration programmes, both at graduate and at mid-management level, come with potential pitfalls. Many of the HR leaders whom I interviewed, for example, recognized the

**Table 4.1**  Examples of graduate acceleration programmes and their defining characteristics

| **Organization 1** | |
| --- | --- |
| Desired outcome | Close to manager level on completion<br>Participants tested in their first role after the acceleration programme<br>Are they up to it? |
| Target group | Graduates (with previous summer internship at organization)<br>Best 2–3 candidates from graduate programme chosen for accelerated track |
| Assessment | Rigorous assessment including cognitive and personality profiling |
| Acceleration approach | Rotation<br>Exposure to all key disciplines, eg finance, HR |
| International exposure | Yes |
| Length | 18 months (2 x 9-month placements) |
| **Organization 2** | |
| Outcome | Manager level on completion |
| Target group | In their mid-20s<br>Best graduates from graduate programme |
| Assessment | |
| Acceleration approach | Lead one project |
| Length | 2 years |
| Support | Career path tools<br>Cultural support |
| **Organization 3** | |
| Outcome | Future leaders |
| Target group | Graduates<br>Most participants multi-lingual |
| Assessment | Tough internal assessments<br>3 days of assessment centres |
| Acceleration approach | Rotation<br>4 rotations of 6 months each.<br>Different markets and functions |
| International exposure | Yes |

(*continued*)

**Table 4.1**   (*Continued*)

| Length | 2 years |
|---|---|
| Support | 6-monthly skills development workshops<br>Mentor |
| **Organization 4** | |
| Outcome | Acceleration |
| Target group | Millennials |
| Assessment | Tough internal assessments<br>3 days of assessment centres |
| Acceleration approach | Special projects<br>Action learning and presentation to senior management |
| Length | 1 year |
| Support | Mentor<br>Sponsor |

danger that the extra input and attention that they give their brightest talent brings. Acceleration does not only create a pool of potential leaders but can also increase a high-potential employee's feelings of entitlement, as well as reduce their loyalty. These young employees are outstanding, and they know that they are. It is probably not surprising that these promising emerging leaders also develop a high level of expectations towards their employers about available opportunities, career support and speed of progression. We will explore millennials' own view of careers in Chapter 10, and in the next chapter we will further delve into the potential pitfalls of acceleration programmes and how to address these.

# Leadership programmes

While graduate programmes seem to predominantly focus on formal six-month rotations over a 12- to 24-month period, middle-management programmes for broadening a future senior leader's experience base are often less structured. This is not surprising, as it is harder to take a high-performing middle manager out of their day job and rotate them across a number of shorter assignments. Furthermore, shorter assignments no longer provide the depth and challenge of experience that a middle manager requires. At middle management, high-potential employees are likely to take on much larger roles where results take longer to deliver. As we will see in the next chapter, parachuting a mid-management high-potential employee into an assignment and taking them out of the role again too quickly may mean that they do not see the impact of their decisions or fail to learn about the longer-term benefits of investing in building a team or strong relationships, both of which are potential derailers for high-potential employees.

As shown in Figure 4.1, there are a range of different solutions that organizations use to add further breadth of experience for their most talented mid-management employees. These range from formal two-year stretch assignments all the way to informal shadowing.

## Stretch assignments and rotational programmes

Rotational programmes still feature in mid-management acceleration efforts; however, only in a few cases are these still the closely defined programmes that we came across for graduate programmes. The preferred way to consciously broaden out a person's experience base at mid-management level seems to be stretch roles that are assigned on an individual basis and not as part of a programme with closely defined start and end dates. These stretch roles tend to be for

**Figure 4.1**   Types of leadership development interventions for increasing breadth of experience

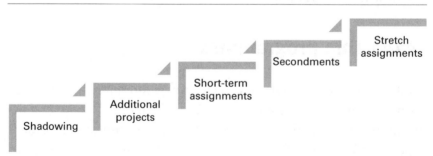

two or three years. In some organizations, the top team's commit-ment to providing mid-management employees with access to pivotal roles is strong enough to allow the HR team to safeguard these roles for development purposes. This ring-fencing of roles is, however, rare and not possible in many organizations. As we will see in the next chapter, many HR leaders have ongoing negotiations with business leaders about whether a role should be held open for an emerging leader for development purposes or whether it should go to a tried and tested applicant, as is often the preference of business leaders who want low-risk appointments for important roles.

At the other end of the spectrum are organizations that do not actively broaden an emerging leader's experience by posting them to a new role. Instead, these organizations are setting an upper limit on how long someone can stay in role. It is probably not warranted to call these arrangements rotational programmes, but they do reflect a type of rotation policy, albeit on a much slower schedule. Rather than actively rotating leaders through pivotal roles, these organizations want to ensure that emerging leaders do not become stale in their roles and stipulate that a person must move on after a maximum of four or five years in the role.

## Secondments

Another way to develop leaders, one that seems to be used more frequently in the public sector, is to second a high-potential employee to another organization. This approach can be very effective where a high-potential employee has spent most of their career in one organization. Secondments are typically time-limited to one or two years and allow an emerging leader to experience a different work environment and a different business model. Secondments are often to non-competing organizations, which means that they allow the high-potential employee to experience a different industry sector. As we saw in Chapter 3, while it may be tempting to stay in a familiar environment as we know how to get things done, it is only when we move outside our comfort zone that are we forced to learn new ways of solving problems and delivering results.

## Shorter assignments

For jobs at mid-management level it can take two to three years before the impact of the actions and decisions that the high-potential employee has taken in the role become apparent. As a result, longer assignments at this level are preferable. However, where such longer rotations or stretch assignments are not feasible, some organizations consider shorter assignments, up to six months, for some of their high-potential employees. It is often a way of broadening a person's horizon and exposing them to either a new country, new customer base or new markets. While the learning may not be as impactful as a two-year assignment, these assignments are nevertheless beneficial and bring several advantages. First, individuals tend to stay in their current role, which means that there is no requirement for difficult negotiations about which department will be carrying the headcount for the high-potential individual. It may also make it easier for an individual to try out a new role. If things don't work out they can always return to their former role. Short-term assignments offer an opportunity to 'dip in a toe'. They may also suit high-potential employees who are not able to move away from their home location for a longer period due to family commitments.

These short-term assignments are rarely in areas that are core to the business though, as too little time is available on a short assignment to get someone ready to contribute in a meaningful way. As a result, these roles don't tend to be as senior and impactful as longer assignments, and the high-potential employee is unlikely to be able to learn how to make key decisions and to experience the impact of these decisions.

## Additional stretch projects

As an alternative to fixed-term assignments, we often find stretch projects that someone takes on in addition to their main job. These projects often provide access to senior management. They allow emerging leaders to develop themselves and at the same time add value to the business. Often, these additional stretch projects are part of formal leadership development programmes that use project-based work as a means of development. As with all roles, the secret to making stretch projects a success is finding a meaningful project for someone to work on. Examples could be involvement in organizational change programmes, innovation initiatives, or anything that the senior management team has identified as important. These projects must be business-critical and provide access to senior decision-makers.

## Shadowing

> I will only develop and increase my competence if I make mistakes. I cannot learn from successes. If we have a culture where I work alongside a senior sparring partner, then I can see how they deal with difficult situations or rescue a project. I can learn from this interaction.
>
> Torsten Schneider, Director Human Resources,
> Luther Rechtsanwaltsgesellschaft

The final form of providing breadth of experience is the least disruptive. It is based on the 20 per cent of the 70:20:10 model – learning from others. It is about work shadowing, which sometimes forms part of a more structured leadership development programme. While it may have less developmental value than giving something a go yourself, in some situations it may be the only way to gain additional experiences. Shadowing a board meeting at the very top of an organization may be a great opportunity to gain insight into interactions at the most senior level. This experience may not be available any other way. Alternatively, it can mean working closely with an expert or more senior colleague on a project with the aim of learning from the other person. In some business sectors, for example the legal or the professional services sector, where teams are made up of people at different seniority levels, these approaches to development are common. By being able to see a more experienced colleague in action, the high-potential employee can learn what works and what doesn't work. For these arrangements to work well, a level of trust between the sparring partners helps to create a climate where learning can be accelerated through meaningful feedback, the ability to ask open questions and to experiment with different approaches. Behavioural modelling has been found to be an effective leadership development tool.[5]

## Other approaches

Other less frequently mentioned approaches to experiential learning include one-off solutions that can be used outside of official acceleration programmes. Examples of these are outdoor activities, which can be useful ways of increasing specific leadership skills such as teamworking or risk-taking. Outdoor activities focus on process rather than on conveying new knowledge or skills. As a result, teams may work better after attending an outdoor programme as the team has gained increased insights about how it interacts in unusual situations. These programmes are unlikely to generate changes to individual behaviour though.

Future search is another experiential learning solution and is an effective alternative to a much more formal and structured conference or meeting. This approach is based on principles of participation and collaborative enquiry. Often conducted as a three-day event with around 50 to 60 participants from different business units, functions and seniority levels in an organization, future search events address a big issue that the organization is likely to face in future and must find solutions to. The group develop insights and increased understanding by working across the organization and its multiple perspectives. Exploring the past and current practices through the use of photos, brochures and any other relevant artefacts helps to identify values for the future. The group is encouraged to reflect on their learning and to create a desirable vision of the future. Participants also take away important insights for themselves, their teams and work units.[6]

Conversational learning is yet another form of experiential learning. It is a way for teams to increase their effectiveness through being able to openly discuss their experiences in the team (concrete experience), which requires a climate of trust and openness. The team then jointly reflects on these experiences (reflective observation) and integrates the various experiences and points of views into a shared view to help the team become more aligned (abstract conceptualization). This serves as a foundation to agree and execute specific actions (active experimentation).[7]

Future search and conversational learning contain significant elements of reflection, an important concept that we will explore in more detail in Chapter 7.

## In practice: leadership development programmes for acceleration

We have just launched a flagship leadership programme. It is called 'Leading Across Boundaries'. It is aimed at people who are more than five years away from C-level but who have aspirations. We introduce them to a broader definition of leadership and to the concept of the enterprise. We accelerate their journey as enterprise leaders. They do a few cohort projects. Our executive committee select the cohort projects and review them later. We help the participants to choose good projects; projects that are stretching for them. They learn to work with different people in different parts of the business. They also do individual development projects and have individual career conversations. We use diagnostics and identify the areas where people have less capability. The diagnostics also help to raise self-awareness about the impact of their leadership style. We have a talent review process with the individual and their line manager about their aspirations and potential.

Jennifer Duvalier, Non-Executive Director, Mitie plc, Guardian Media Group plc, Royal College of Arts

When it comes to stretch assignments, we don't talk about roles but about processes and projects. Which projects are deemed to be stretch assignments depends on what areas we are currently focusing on and what organizational phase we find ourselves in. This determines what special projects we have.

Ursula Schwarzenbart, Head of Talent Development & Diversity Management, Daimler AG

# Assigning critical job assignments

Where organizations run formal rotation or acceleration program- mes, either for early or mid-career talent, participants are expected to go through an official selection process. Participants either apply or self-nominate for the programme. In some organizations, employees may be put forward for a programme by their managers. Following the initial selection process, participants then tend to go through psychometric profiling and a development centre. We will take a closer look at the challenges and solutions to assessing potential and the associated psychometric assessment in the next chapter.

Talent management conversations tend to form part of most acceleration programmes, be they formal or informal. They can take place either before or after a formal assessment process, and in some organizations, they replace a formal selection process. It is in these meetings that career ambitions are explored, development plans established and the type of experience that a high-potential employee may benefit from discussed. The next step is to find suit- able stretch roles. This may involve some 'out-of-the-box' thinking to identify development opportunities. Talent management conver- sations often not only include the high-potential employee and a member of the HR development team, but also the high-potential employee's manager or their mentor. Involving line managers beyond the initial talent management conversation in broader development activities, such as becoming mentors, identifying high-potentials or overseeing stretch projects increases the likelihood of accelerated development becoming part of an organization's culture rather than it being perceived as an HR initiative.[8]

As we saw earlier on, in many cases stretch assignments are assig- ned on an individual basis and often as the result of the high-potential employee's initiative and the organization's desire to develop the person further. In these situations, there is not always a lot of process in place. The benefit of a more informal approach is that the organi- zation can not only look at the needs of the emerging leader but also the needs of the wider team that this leader is considered for. The HR team can ask questions such as:

- Is the leader of the team capable of taking on more people with development needs?
- Does the team already have a high-potential employee who is assigned to their role as a development opportunity?
- Is the team large enough to be able to absorb a team member who is taking on a role as a stretch assignment with relatively little knowledge in the area?

Depending on the answers to such questions, the organization may decide not to add anyone to the role as a development opportunity, and instead assign a more experienced person. It also allows the organization to react to the needs of the business, such as maternity cover or a vacancy due to a recent resignation. Where the process is informal, the organization can move fast. This is often necessary, as high-visibility roles can come up at short notice due to organizational change or crisis situations.

Where there is no application process or where the appointment to the role happens through tapping someone with potential on the shoulder, a business leader's subjective assessment of the high-potential employee replaces the assessment process. As a result, candidates are more likely to come from the appointing business leader's network. While this makes for a very flexible process, as we will see in Chapter 9 informal processes that rely on a manager's personal network are liable to in-group favouritism and make it much harder to combat bias and a lack of diversity in appointments for critical, career-enhancing roles.

## What makes leadership development programmes effective?

Each organization must choose the approach that works best for them, considering culture, available resources and desired outcomes. To increase the effectiveness of any leadership development effort, organizations must ensure that their leadership programmes are linked to business strategy, both current and future. Future-proofing the content of programmes will ensure that these programmes deliver the leaders that an organization will need in five years' time. Programmes must also be regularly reviewed to ensure that they are still aligned with overall business strategy. Any programme must also be based on a rigorous analysis of current leadership development needs.

When it comes to selecting participants for programmes, it is important that candidates who are chosen for accelerated leadership development input are also part of the organization's succession plan.[9] Organizations must find the balance between developing a cohort of leaders who are agile and well-rounded enough to take on any role in future with the organization's need to fill critical roles in the near to medium future.

As we already saw earlier on in this chapter, effective on-the-job learning requires personal reflection. Therefore, any successful acceleration programme requires adequate support infrastructures that help the accelerated leader take a step back and learn from the experiences they have gained. Line managers, mentors and sponsors play an important role here. This infrastructure should not be regarded as nice to have but should form part of any official programme. We will explore this topic in more detail in Chapter 8. Finally, organizations need leaders who are willing to invest time in developing emerging talent. These talent builders should be celebrated as role models and rewarded with additional recognition and promotion opportunities.

## Summary

As we saw in this chapter, many organizations provide job rotation for their most promising talent predominantly at two career points – early-career and mid-management level. The benefits of breadth of experience provided at early-career and middle-management level differ. Early broadening out, often achieved through a series of six-month rotations across different parts of an organization and frequently also across different countries, provides a young professional with an organization-wide view, a can-do attitude and a stronger network of contacts right from the start. Introducing breadth at mid-management level, by taking on two or three longer assignments in strategically important areas, allows the high-potential individual to lead an important part of the business as the head of a business unit or a manager of managers. This provides an understanding of running critical parts of the organization, of turning into an enterprise leader, taking big decisions and seeing the impact of these decisions.

Early-career programmes tend to be based on the 70:20:10 approach, where experiential learning through exposure to a series of roles is supported by mentors and further supplemented with formal training. These programmes tend to run for between 18 months and 2 years.

Middle-management programmes tend to be more varied and overall less formalized. While some organizations offer formal programmes, unlike graduate programmes, these programmes tend to focus on project work rather than regular job rotations. Generally, middle managers are either assigned to a two- or three-year role that has been selected as a stretch assignment to fill some blank spaces on their CV, or they take on a stretch project in addition to their day job. These stretch projects are often chosen by the organization's top team and focus on topics of strategic importance. The organization's executive team review the emerging leaders' work on these projects, which provides much needed visibility. Alternatives are secondments, shadowing, or shorter solutions such as future search or conversational learning.

When it comes to getting access to the various types of programmes and assignments, organizations use a variety of processes. The most formal are selection processes, including psychometric profiling and in some cases assessment centres. At the other end of the spectrum, there are informal conversations. In these situations, personal networks and initiative help secure access to stretch roles or projects. While these informal processes allow an organization maximum flexibility, they also reduce the diversity of candidates that tend to get access to stretch roles, as senior leaders rely on their personal networks to fill roles.

## Organizational design tips

- **Secure senior management buy-in.** Organizations that have the buy-in of their senior management teams achieve better results, as roles can be ring-fenced for development purposes and senior leaders are actively involved in project-based work to help develop emerging leaders. Furthermore, involving line managers in the various elements of the leadership programme, such as acting as a mentor, identifying high-potential employees or overseeing stretch projects, means that the acceleration programme is more likely to create a genuine learning culture rather than being perceived as an HR initiative.

- **Remove process barriers early.** Job rotations and cross-departmental moves can be hampered by questions over the length of an assignment or which department carries the headcount for the high-potential employee. Furthermore, managers may not be willing to let good people go. Address these potential barriers early to ensure that job rotations do not fail due to organizational red tape and incentivize managers to become talent builders.

- **Maximize experiential learning opportunities.** Experiential learning is not only about experiencing a new situation. For effective experiential learning, build opportunities for personal reflection and the ability to actively experiment with new learning into the process. On formal programmes this can be achieved by including reflection elements. With informal acceleration efforts, mentors and coaches can be tasked with encouraging the high-potential employee to actively reflect on their experiences.

- **Offer a variety of experiential learning options.** While two- or three-year stretch roles may be the most effective way of introducing more breadth to a high-potential's experience base, consider the full range of available options, including secondments, shorter assignments and shadowing. This will allow you to cater for the needs of different high-potential employees and therefore increase the number of employees who benefit from broadening out their experience base.

- **Have a formal selection process.** Formal selection processes, even if light-touch, are better than no process at all. The more formal the process, the more likely it is that a broad range of high-potential employees will have access to career-enhancing stretch projects and roles. Where little or no process is in place, it is more likely that only people within the recruiting business leader's network will be considered for roles. And the temptation of appointing in the business leader's own image will be greater in the absence of formal checks and balances.

## Individual coaching tips

- **Look for programmes.** Not all development programmes are widely advertised. Ask HR or your manager about available acceleration and rotation programmes. Furthermore, find out what informal processes exist. If your business unit does not offer any programmes, other business units may. Check if you are eligible to apply for these programmes.

- **Use your initiative and network.** If no formal programmes exist, create your own opportunities by using your initiative and network. Talk to colleagues and mentors to explore how other people in the organization have managed to secure interesting projects and roles. If you cannot find an opportunity to gain important experiences, consider looking outside the organization. You could take on a role at a local community group or a charity.

- **Consider shadowing.** Explore if you can gain additional experience by shadowing a senior member of your organization, either officially or through carefully observing how they behave or interact with others. We can learn a lot by observing both effective and ineffective behaviours in the senior managers around us.

- **Communicate.** Be at the top of someone's mind when a stretch role or project comes up by keeping your career stakeholders up to date about what experiences you are looking for. Don't be afraid to remind them occasionally about your goals. Be ready to ask. And then ask again. Sometimes it takes a little bit of time for the right role to come up.

# Notes

1 Kolb, D (1984) *Experiential Learning: Experience as the source of learning and development*, Prentice Hall, Englewood Cliffs, NJ

2 Lombardo, MM and Eichinger, RW (1996) *The Career Architect Development Planner*, Lominger, Minneapolis, MN

3 Kolb, D (1984) *Experiential Learning: Experience as the source of learning and development*, Prentice Hall, Englewood Cliffs, NJ

4  Clark, RW, Threeton, MD and Ewing, JC (2010) The potential of experiential learning models and practices in career and technical teacher education, *Journal of Career and Technical Education*, 25, pp 46–62

5  Adams, AB, Kayes, DC and Kolb, DA (2004) Experiential learning in teams, Working Paper ORBH 12/13/04, Department of Organizational Behavior, Weatherhead School of Management, Case Western Reserve University

6  Lewis, LH and Williams, CJ (1994) Experiential learning: Past and present, *New Directions for Adult and Continuing Education*, Summer 1994, Jossey-Bass, available from https://eric.ed.gov/?id=EJ492388

7  Adams, AB, Kayes, DC and Kolb, DA (2004) Experiential learning in teams, Working Paper ORBH 12/13/04, Department of Organizational Behavior, Weatherhead School of Management, Case Western Reserve University

8  Groves, KS (2006) Integrating leadership development and succession planning best practices, *Journal of Management Development*, 26, pp 239–60

9  Leskiw, S-L and Singh, P (2007) Leadership development: Learning from best practices, *Leadership & Organization Development Journal*, 28, pp 444–64

# Navigating the pitfalls of acceleration

05

## Incomplete learning and burnout

*When leaders are overstretched, mistakes happen that can cost the organization a lot of money. This also impacts the mood of the team that works for the leader. Especially in uncertain times, teams need leaders who can create calm, trust and stability, otherwise the team cannot perform at its best.*

ALEXANDRA AUBART, DIRECTOR ORGANIZATIONAL
DEVELOPMENT, LSG LUFTHANSA SERVICE HOLDING AG

*You can do a super stretch role followed by another super stretch role but then you should only do a stretch role. You must be able to dial it up and down. This allows you to pull together all the stretch and learning from it. If you don't dial down, then you are so far out of your comfort zone that you don't know what it is any more. You need to pull it all together for greater insights.*

JENNIFER DUVALIER, NON-EXECUTIVE DIRECTOR, MITIE PLC,
GUARDIAN MEDIA GROUP PLC, ROYAL COLLEGE OF ARTS

## The dark side of acceleration

There are numerous benefits to accelerating a leader's career journey, as we saw in Chapter 1. Among other things, it prepares the high-potential employee for leadership in a volatile and uncertain business world. It fosters innovation and engages millennials who are keen to develop fast. But there is also a dark side to accelerated development, which organizations must address proactively if they want to reap the full benefits of high-potential employees' faster career progression. Accelerated development is demanding, requiring a move every 18 months to 3 years, depending on the level of seniority. Most of these job moves bring substantial changes in responsibility. It is not unusual for a high-potential employee to move from an assignment abroad to a turnaround project where they are closing significant parts of an organization's operation, only to then move on to a change management project where they have been tasked with implementing an organization-wide business process re-engineering initiative. Such moves come with risks for both the individual, such as personal burnout, failure or incomplete learning, as well as risks for the organization, such as wrong business decisions and significant financial losses.

We differentiate between internal and external derailment. Internal derailment leads to an implosion and burnout of the high-potential employee. External derailment refers to an explosion of the high-potential employee where their actions cause substantial damage.[1]

In this chapter we will explore the potential dangers of accelerated leadership development for a high-potential leader that must be managed carefully. The In Practice box below illustrates some of these dangers well:

- burnout;
- not learning how to fail;
- a lack of people skills;
- becoming a one-dimensional leader;
- unrealistic expectations of career progression.

---

### In practice: the dangers of accelerated leadership development

With acceleration there is a danger of having immature leaders. It takes time to become a leader. People need time to adapt. The lack of maturity is reflected in a person's leadership style. People become uni-dimensional and very focused. Empathy and emotional skills can fall by the wayside.

Dr Ursula Schütze-Kreilkamp, Head of Group HR
Development & Group Executives, Deutsche Bahn AG

In future, people will join organizations because of the organization's purpose and its goals. To drive vision and purpose we need truly inspirational, vulnerable leaders who can create followership and build strong teams by sharing what they have learned on their own path to leadership. Simply accelerating leaders, moving them as fast as possible through positions, is not enough. Leaders need to be able to experience the consequence of their actions, they need to be allowed to learn to become a role model. It is not about speed; it is about giving back and shaping our culture. We aim for a work environment where people can be the best they can be.

Vera Gramkow, Global Head of Talent & Performance
Development, Bayer AG

Some team members have the capacity to move up and keep going but that is very rare. Some need to move sideways to consolidate – many do some lateral moves to broaden their knowledge. We cannot always set out a programme of job moves; this progression is different for everyone. We carefully monitor how they are performing. Individuals tell us when they need more time. Sometimes they find something they are really interested in, such as an operational, commercial, finance or HR role. We work with them; it's a two-way conversation.

Brendan Toomey, Vice President, Human Resources
Asia Pacific, Hilton

There is a danger that, if we start preparing promising talent for senior roles too early, we don't consider any alternative career paths for this person. If they haven't reached the role we had in mind for them within a certain timeframe, we regard the person as a failure. Instead, we should engage in a personalized development process.

Torsten Schneider, Director Human Resources,
Luther Rechtsanwaltsgesellschaft

## Steering clear of burnout

The following quote is a powerful personal account of the pressures that high-potential leaders can face during stretch assignments. It describes well the price that may have to be paid for an accelerated career and the exceptional learning it can provide:

This was my first job with a child. ... I didn't see my daughter awake during the week for several months, and I was working all the hours, every weekend, so had no time to connect with her (or anyone else). I'm up for leaning in – I've done it my whole career – and I relished the challenge and the brief I'd been given, but the personal cost was no longer acceptable to me in my new context. ... It was also the first time I had a big team. I was putting too much pressure on not just myself but on my team as well by accelerating the size and speed of change too aggressively. It was a very short-term tactic. You have to dial up and dial down. Maybe you need that third year. In Year 1 you work out what to do, in Year 2 you do it and in Year 3 you embed the change to ensure that it sustains when you move on. My challenge is, how do I maintain my energy over time to last throughout my career so that I can be the best I can be for my work, for myself and for my family? It is also about how you approach a role. My new role is at a different level. I deal with really big stuff and also with really small stuff; and the really small stuff can become really big stuff if you are not on top of it. I've had to become a ninja at prioritization of time and task. You have to be able to create a clear picture of the future for your team, and of the journey you are asking them to join you on; you have to be able to do focused think-ing on the big issues, without the day-to-day of the operation becoming all-consuming; and you have to be effective in a world of back-to-back meetings, every day, at asking the right questions, coming to the right conclusions and making the right decisions, all in the moment so your team is enabled and empowered to deliver. You need to be at the top of your game all the time to do that consistently well.

Bella Vuillermoz, Director,
Property Service Group, Sky UK

Burnout is often associated with having too much to do. My early research work focused on work overload, a phenomenon often encountered by high-potential employees.[2] Work overload is damag-ing for health and well-being as an employee finds themselves in a situation where they have more and more to do, which means that they have to fall back onto their reserve capacities, a strategy that will, over time, lead to decreased performance and exhaustion.[3] Furthermore, if we have ever-increasing amounts of work pile up, we lose control over our jobs. We are no longer able to complete the tasks set for us by the organization. This further exacerbates the situation and may lead to eventual breakdown in task performance and to burnout.[4] Another factor that may contribute to burnout is the increasing inability to appreciate one's talents and abilities in the face of mounting and eventually unmanageable amounts of work and responsibility. This may lead to a lack of self-belief, which in turn can lead to a further loss of feeling that we are in control.[5] It is easy to see how a high-potential employee who has been appointed to a new high-stretch role, after having just completed another stretch role, can easily fall into a situation where they are drawing on already depleted reserve capacity.

Burnout should not be an individual's issue to deal with alone. Most driven high-potential employees want to do well and fulfil their potential. High-potential individuals are therefore unlikely to turn down roles that they have been offered and that they deem to be career-enhancing. They may fear that, if they turn down a role, they may no longer be regarded as high-potential and that they may not be approached with new opportunities in the future. This is not an unwarranted concern. When organizations tap a perceived high-potential individual on the shoulder and offer a stretch role, the high-potential individual's willingness to take on the role is often interpreted as a 'can-do' attitude and courage to take on challenges.

Furthermore, several organizations put the onus on their high-potential employees to put themselves forward for acceleration programmes. Some organizations are expecting their employees to take risks and they assess their risk-taking appetite by using a self-nomination process. A high-potential employee may therefore feel that they need to keep putting themselves forward for new challenges.

HR, business leaders, and organizations more broadly, must carefully balance a desire for ambitious leaders who have an appetite for ever-increasing stretch roles on the one hand, and the need to take responsibility for how to pace these high-potential employees' career development on the other. Organizations must recognize the need for balance. Bursts of activity and personal sacrifice must be balanced with periods of consolidation and dialling down. There is a fine balance between too much and too little acceleration. As we saw in Chapter 2, for junior roles a good length of time in role seems to be 18 months, for mid-management roles it is two to three years, and for senior roles three to four years. These are averages, and it is vital to have open conversations with a high-potential employee about their personal circumstances.

Furthermore, organizations need a good understanding of how much stretch each role represents for a high-potential employee. Moving to a more senior role in a different function and possibly also a different country is likely to contain too many stretch elements. It is easy to underestimate the demands of boundary-spanning roles, such as taking on a significantly more senior role or moving abroad.

## Regular reviews and viable alternatives

To assess whether the balance between stretch and consolidation is right, organizations should provide formal windows for reflection that can help an accelerated leader determine whether an accelerated leadership path is still the right choice. If a high-potential employee is no longer committed to an accelerated leadership route, the organization should help to provide alternatives. During these check-ins, it is important that the high-potential employee understands that dialling down or even taking a temporary step back is a legitimate alternative. Equally, finding an alternative progression path other than becoming a leader is important. If these alternatives are not provided, high-potentials may not feel that it is legitimate to leave their current trajectory, which will make burnout or derailment more likely. Another potential consequence of not being able to review their current career trajectory is that high-potential employees will regard departure from the organization as their only way out, as they may fear that their reputation will be negatively affected if they express a desire to dial down or to pursue a different career path. As we saw in Chapter 4, organizations tend to use psychometric profiling to get a better understanding of the underlying potential of a star performer. However, such assessments may only prove accurate for the next one or two roles. To avoid future derailment or burnout, it is important for the organization to have regular conversations with the high-potentials, alongside occasional reassessment of potential.

## Time for stillness

When the interviewees talked about consolidation, it became clear that the ability to be still and step back also provides the breathing space that busy executives need to manage heavy workloads and to prevent burnout. Senior executives have learned about the value of stepping back, reflection or practising meditation. It is probably not surprising that concepts such as mindfulness have found great resonance in organizations. If we can help emerging leaders learn the benefit of stillness and moments of conscious 'time out', we can equip them with the staying power to last them throughout their entire career. Sometimes, these moments of 'time out' may be a short moment, a deliberate stepping back or a short sabbatical. While not often listed as a leadership capability necessary for the VUCA world and rarely enshrined in organization's competency frameworks, teaching emerging leaders the value of time out, of stepping back and recharging batteries, is nevertheless a skill worth investing in.

### In practice: the benefits of slowing down for senior leaders

I live one hour from the office. I commute. I used to jam my commute full of calls. Then when I got home my head was full of work calls and I snapped at the kids. I had to take myself away and calm down. Now I spend that time reflecting: what are my issues at work? I have always played competitive team sports. But two or three years ago I started running again. I often come back from a run now and jot things down straight away. I get some of my best ideas this way. The pace is fast, it's 24/7 and we are online all the time. Proliferation of work smartphones makes access to work e-mail too accessible. We need to figure out how and what to do to switch off. Either as active time or time with the family. We need to learn to switch off. We need self-awareness 2.0; where you evolve from knowing yourself to understanding how your behaviour impacts others.

Stephen Caulfield, Vice President Global Field Services & GM Dell Bratislava, Dell EMC Global Services

We are a very driven organization. Sometimes people can lose their safety valve, such as going home, taking a break and going on holiday. This increases the danger of burnout. We do well-being work, stress counselling and yoga. We have a lot of communications about these topics. When people are floating back in from holidays they often say, 'While I was away, I was thinking we need to do this differently...'. We need more of this reflection and enable it to happen.

HR Leader, Global Organization

Reflection is something I do intrinsically. I ask myself, 'What could I have done better?', 'How do I leverage this learning elsewhere?', 'What would make things more efficient for the organization?' We have 360-degree feedback and I have learned from the feedback that I have received from colleagues about what I can do differently and what I am good at. It's about taking time. We must build in time for relaxation, rest and reflection. More recently, I have started practising mindfulness and meditation and I find that I am making connections or think of something new when I meditate. It is also important to get enough sleep. When I wind down, sometimes things will occur to me and I feel a renewed energy to take on challenges.

Robert Baker, Senior Partner, Mercer

## Balance

Organizations must find the right balance between the amount of drive they expect from their employees and the amount of support they provide. As Figure 5.1 shows, the balance between these two elements will determine the likelihood of a high-potential employee on an accelerated career track experiencing burnout.

If we expect self-driven individuals to continually put themselves forward for stretch roles, we must provide higher levels of support if we are to avoid burnout and derailment. We will look at the role of support in Chapter 8. A high amount of support will reduce the danger of burnout in times of accelerated career progression. However, in some cases it may also mean that people become over-reliant on the support and ultimately fail. Getting the balance right requires

**Figure 5.1** Finding the right balance for accelerated leadership development

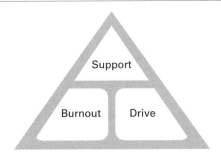

regular, candid conversations between the organization and the high-potential employee to understand a high-potential employee's appetite for more stretch. It also requires a more nuanced definition of talent. Only because a high-potential employee is currently not ready to take on another stretch role does not mean that they are no longer ambitious and therefore no longer a rising star.

This also takes us back to the time–cost–quality equation that we explored in Chapter 2. Accelerated leadership development is about carefully balancing a number of factors such as drive, support and burnout at an individual level, and cost, time, quality and scope at an organizational level. In Chapter 6, we will examine the role of careful evaluation to help us get this balance right and to increase our return on risk.

## *Allowing learning from failure*

Taking on increasingly challenging roles that continually stretch a person's ability increases the risk of failure. While being able to validate one's existing views of the world in a new country and adapting one's problem-solving approaches to an unfamiliar environment is highly developmental, there is a fine line between enough stretch and too much stretch. It is not only *actual* failure in role that poses a danger to an individual's brand and their future career success, but also the risk of *not learning how to deal with failure* or what to do when things go wrong.

## In practice: learning from failure

The danger of accelerated development is more than people failing. It is the danger of a self-fulfilling prophecy. People are put in roles and they succeed as we give them extra support. If they mess up, then we move them on to the next role. Organizations can become blind to the outcomes.

Uxio Malvido, Head of Talent Acquisition, Engagement & Inclusion,
Lafarge Holcim

With acceleration there is a danger that people will crash and burn when there is a problem. This is because they have always done well and because they expect to know what to do, but then they don't know what to do and they don't have the networks to tap into to help them. People who have never failed will fail one day. How will the person and the organization react then?

Stephen Caulfield, Vice President Global Field Services & GM Dell
Bratislava, Dell EMC Global Services

We want people to have learning agility. We don't want them to be completely accepting. We want them to challenge. We want people to do something with their new knowledge and demonstrate risk-taking and courage of their own conviction. People must be able to deal with failure: 'I believe in my heart it's the right thing but oops, that didn't work. What can I take from this and learn?' It's about the ability to take risks and stand by your decision. There are very few leaders who are happy to do this and very few who are willing to go beyond the confines of their role, so the questioning of processes and people is often not a strength of our leaders. How do we create this environment? It's not easy. We put all our energy into people who have courage and strong communication skills. We give them access to bigger roles.

Brendan Toomey, Vice President, Human Resources
Asia Pacific, Hilton

High-potential employees, like everyone else, benefit from learning from failure. And with stretch roles or projects that require difficult decision-making in complex or ambiguous situations, the risk of the high-potential employee making mistakes is increased. And it is not only the inexperienced high-potential employee who makes mistakes and fails. Research has shown that top teams, frequently faced with complex situations, regularly make mistakes and fail, too.[6, 7]

In a new role there is likely to be trial and error as the emerging leader is trying to learn the ropes. However, failure is the ultimate, most traumatic trial and error experience.[8] Feelings of guilt, self-blame and embarrassment are often reported in connection with failure.[9]

Organizations' desires for their high-potential employees to succeed may mean that these promising star performers are not allowed to fail. Instead, when high-potential employees start to struggle in a new role, the organization may be inclined to give this person support as they are deemed to be a future leader. When this additional support does not pay off, the high-potential may be moved to a new role. An organization's desire for their star performers to do well may make the organization blind to early signs of failure. Of course, any person transitioning to a new role should be given reasonable onboarding support, particularly if the new role is a stretch role in an unfamiliar area. However, an over-reliance on support may mean that it is the support and no longer the underlying potential that is making an emerging leader succeed. The question must always be: is this transitional support or is a person being propped up through the additional support? This assessment will have to be made carefully and take into consideration all aspects of a role and the emerging leader. If an emerging leader feels that admitting problems in the role will end their career, they are less likely to seek help and instead will continue to struggle on until it may be too late. On the other hand, if we give star performers an aura of infallibility, then we risk continuing their accelerated leadership development journey without critically evaluating the results they have delivered.

## Reflection

As we saw in Chapter 4, learning from experience is most effective when time is made available to reflect on an experience. This allows a high-potential employee to make sense of a situation and extract general lessons learned that can be applied to future situations. When organizations allow time for such reflection and actively encourage and support it, it will increase the likelihood of reflection taking place. It has been found that where high-potential employees are redeployed with little or no transition time after a failing project, reflection on what went wrong is much less likely to take place.[10] It is harder in these situations to articulate and make sense of the personal failure. This brings us back to consolidation of learning and dwell time, a concept that we have already seen is important in reducing the likelihood of burnout. Dwell time means that an emerging leader can make time for reflection, the practice of taking a step back and looking back at recent experiences to be able to learn from them. This allows an emerging leader to take in all the learning from a stretch role and decreases the risk of incomplete learning and failing in a future role. We will take a closer look at reflection in Chapter 7.

## Developing people skills

Knowing how to fail is in part knowing *who* to ask for help. Often, accelerated leaders have not built the networks they need to help them through a difficult situation. We will come back to the importance of having the right networks in Chapter 8. Furthermore, too much focus on the task at hand will not allow enough time to focus on building strong relationships with people. An accelerated leader may also believe that they don't need others as they have succeeded without the help of others so far.

It is not only the accelerated leader who suffers when they encounter a difficult situation that threatens to derail them. Often, accelerated leaders are placed in management roles where they have other people reporting to them. If the leader is on the verge of failing in their role, this is likely to have a knock-on effect on their team, which is unlikely to perform at its best with a struggling manager in place.

People skills seem to be a skill set that causes significant concerns with accelerated leadership development; it was mentioned by most of the interviewees. This is not surprising as being able to deliver results with and through other people is core to any organization's success. There is a danger that accelerated leaders are lacking an understanding that people need to be included in the decision-making process to create buy-in and generate excitement. Often, accelerated leaders are bright and have succeeded without the help of others until now. If an accelerated leader has relied on their problem-solving capabilities without needing the input of others, they may regard consultation and inclusion of others, along with listening and trying to win others over to their idea, as a waste of time and instead focus on solving problems themselves. As a result, the accelerated leader may not become the talent builder that organizations need their leaders to be in order to ensure the next generation of young talent is bought into the organization's vision, and that they are engaged and developed.

## Rewarding good people skills

Along with evaluating business outcomes, organizations must hold their high-potential employees to account over the impact of their leadership style on other people. Using 360-degree feedback, for example, can be a powerful tool to raise self-awareness and develop emotionally self-aware and inspirational leaders who can create working environments of trust, co-creation and innovation.

Furthermore, recognizing the first move to a people-management position as a stretch assignment in itself, organizations can support an emerging leader through people-management skills training.[11] Finally, mentors, line-managers, HR and anyone working with the high-potential leader to support their accelerated development, must ensure that the high-potential employee understands the importance of people skills and of building a strong network of contacts. They must encourage the emerging leader to invest time in building these skills and networks even if there is a temptation to put all energies into business results.

## *Creating well-rounded leaders*

As we saw in Chapter 1, leadership qualities of successful leaders in the VUCA world are broad and include a variety of capabilities, such as openness to change, being inquisitive and learning continually, personal reflections, creating visions for the future and inspiring others.

Developing these qualities seems to be a fine balancing act between moving high-potential employees between stretch assignments at speed and at the same time giving them enough time to pick up on the nuances and broader context of some of these roles, which allow them to become fully rounded leaders. If a high-potential employee focuses on delivering business results in a minimum of time, there are elements of a role that they may miss out on as these are strictly speaking not core of getting to the desired outcome. They may decide to ignore and not actively engage with:

- all the facets and nuances of a role, such as the less exciting process and systems elements of a fast-paced turnaround role;
- the benefits of adapting leadership styles and being able to move from operating in high-octane stretch roles to being a successful steady-state leader;
- working effectively cross-culturally and taking time to fully explore a new culture and learning how to operate effectively in it; or
- getting to know all the stakeholders in the wider ecosystem of a project and not only the most important decision-makers.

While these factors may not be strictly necessary to get a specific task at hand done, continually missing out on these finer nuances of a role may eventually hamper the accelerated leader's ability to gain an appreciation of how to become truly effective and achieve truly outstanding results in difficult situations. And it is not only personal effectiveness that may be hampered. Focusing exclusively on completing tasks rather than taking in the richness of a role also means that a leader is going to miss out on developing as a rounded leader who has lived, who can tell inspiring stories and who has personal lessons to share. It is this roundedness that makes a leader human, trustworthy and their vision inspiring, an important leadership capability for the VUCA world, as we saw in Chapter 1.

A final danger of moving people on too fast is that they tend not to get the experience of seeing the impact of their decisions play out. By the time the results of the accelerated leader's decisions and actions bear fruit, or not, the emerging leader may have already moved on. There is a need, however, for leaders to see whether their decisions led to the desired outcomes or not. This demands that leaders stay in role long enough.

## Consolidation and the 'third year'

It might sound counter-intuitive advice in a book about accelerated leadership development, but the solution to overcoming burnout, incomplete learning and one-dimensional leaders is consolidation of learning. With this consolidation must come the opportunity to either temporarily or permanently select an alternative to the accelerated track. As we saw earlier on, to facilitate conversations about continuing an accelerated track versus dialling down to consolidate learning requires clear alternatives that are not seen as a failure. It also requires time for reflection and the ability to recharge batteries.

The consolidation of learning must happen both at an organizational as well as an individual level. Organizationally, it is important that at certain points of a career, acceleration is paused in favour of consolidation, which means having the ability to move sideways at the same level of seniority for two or three moves before ascending further to the giddy heights of senior management.

Dwell time may be achieved by taking less challenging side steps rather than high-stretch upward career moves. It may also be achieved by allowing or creating additional time in role. We have already seen that for middle-management roles, for example, the average time in role is two to three years. Several interviewees talked about the benefit of the 'third year'. With Year 1 being spent on learning about the role and Year 2 on delivering in the role, an additional third year at the end of the role will allow a high-potential employee to make sense of the learning in the role as well as experience the impact of their decisions. Reflection is a solution to several of the potential pitfalls that we have explored in this chapter. We will take an in-depth look at the benefits, challenges and solutions for reflection in Chapter 7.

## *Managing expectations and avoiding alienation*

High-potential leaders who are on a formal accelerated development track tend to get a lot of attention. There are assessments, development conversations, projects to be worked on and results to be presented to the organization's senior team. There are mentors and coaches. There is access to leadership courses. While not every organization has a formal programme with all these support elements, high-potential leaders who are nurtured do get more attention than their peers, even if it is only a higher-status mentor or priority access to the best available projects or roles. The reason why we provide this additional support and these enhanced development opportunities is that we see potential in these emerging leaders. And they know, too, that they are valued and as a result they expect faster progression. It is easy to see how preferential treatment and expectations of greatness can lead to a sense of entitlement in the emerging leader. Participants on leadership programmes often expect a promotion to follow soon after the programme is finished or when they return from a stretch assignment. However, organizations are not always able to provide these promotions as quickly as desired by the high-potential employee. It is therefore important that organizations clearly state what an employee can and cannot expect as part of an accelerated leadership development programme. Organizations must manage expectations carefully, which in many cases means that the emerging leader must be clear that while increased development effort is a general commitment to a person's career development, it cannot be a guarantee for a promotion within a certain period of time. Organizations must also be clear that increased developmental investment in a person's career does not absolve the individual from remaining in charge of their career and for taking the initiative to find opportunities, too.

Another potential danger of acceleration is the disengagement and alienation of those who have not been identified as worthy of accelerated leadership development. To keep everyone in the organization engaged, it is vital that organizations:

- Have clear criteria for what makes someone part of a high-potential pool.

- Develop fair and objective selection criteria to show that it is underlying ability and not personal connections that matter.

- Carry out ongoing assessments that make membership of a high-potential programme fluid. Nobody should be anointed as a high-potential employee without the need to continually prove that they are still worthy of being a part of the programme. And everybody should feel that they can access the programme if they show the right characteristics.

- Provide those who have not been selected with high-quality, self-service development opportunities.

## Summary

As we saw in this chapter, accelerated leadership development comes with several pitfalls, the most significant of which are burnout, failing in role and incomplete learning, which can lead to underdeveloped people skills and the failure of becoming a well-rounded leader who understands the finer nuances of any given situation.

It has also become clear that these potential pitfalls can in some cases be exacerbated by the way that some accelerated programmes are designed and structured. Organizations must guard against self-fulfilling prophecies where high-potentials who are placed on an accelerated leadership development track are unduly shielded from failure. Furthermore, organizations must place more emphasis on the impact that the emerging leader has on the people around them. Too often, organizations only measure impact in terms of business objectives achieved and not on engagement levels of the people being led by the high-potential employee. Another reason for incomplete learning is that emerging leaders are moved on from their stretch roles too quickly. As a result, they are no longer in role when the impact of their actions and decisions becomes visible. Experiencing the impact of one's decisions first-hand is, however, vital feedback for the developing leader.

Organizations can further help to make accelerated leadership development programmes more effective for the individual by pacing roles, thus avoiding burnout. And organizations must carefully manage the expectations of their accelerated leaders, the managers of these rising stars and those who are not on an accelerated track, to avoid unrealistic expectations, disappointment and disengagement.

One way to guard against some of these potential pitfalls is to allow periods of consolidation – the opportunity to take a side step or a less challenging role before moving on to the next level or another high-stretch role. At an individual level, high-potential leaders benefit from taking time for personal reflection and organizations can support this reflection process by putting in place formal opportunities to review whether a person still wants to be on an accelerated path or not. We will look more closely at the important role of reflective learning in Chapter 7.

## Organizational design tips

- **Manage expectations from the start.** Be clear that a high-potential employee's participation in an acceleration programme is not guaranteed. The right to be part of the programme must be re-earned on an ongoing basis. Ensure that people continue to take responsibility for their own careers by encouraging them to take ownership of making the right contacts in the organization and for being responsible for 'sourcing' some of their own development opportunities. Be clear that a promotion may not be available upon completion of the programme.

- **Have clear rules about how frequently people move between roles.** A lack of policy can lead to overstretch as people rarely say 'no' to a great opportunity for fear of not being deemed ambitious enough any longer. For junior roles, a good time in role seems to be 18 months to 2 years, for mid-management roles it is two to three years, and for senior roles, three to four years. These are averages, and it is vital to have regular, open conversations with a high-potential employee about their personal circumstances.

- **Focus on outcomes to avoid self-fulfilling prophecies.** Ensure that emerging leaders who are on an accelerated development track deliver expected outcomes to check that they are living up to expectations. Avoid temptations to move an emerging leader on before the real impact of their decisions and actions has become evident.

- **People impact.** Pay attention to an emerging leader's impact on the people around them. We must make good people-management skills as much of a priority for an accelerated leader's development as delivering business results. The impact of an emerging leader's leadership is less easy to assess than business results. Using tools such as engagement surveys or 360-degree feedback can be helpful to establish how effectively the emerging leader is developing as a people manager.

- **Accelerate but provide alternatives.** To ensure that accelerated leaders don't burn out or suffer from incomplete learning, provide viable alternatives to the accelerated development track. Ensure that alternatives, such as moving to a non-accelerated track or taking a side step, are positioned as acceptable choices and not as a failure that marks the end of the emerging leader's career. There is merit in consolidation and dwell time for star performers.

- **Provide support but avoid propping up.** Every person, whether on an accelerated leadership development track or not, must receive adequate support as they transition into a new role, particularly if this role is significantly different from the person's last role. In high-stretch roles, support in the form of a mentor or sponsor may be necessary throughout the assignment. While a 'sink or swim' approach is never a constructive way of identifying future leaders, evaluate carefully if the level of support required by an emerging leader is justified or if it may be a first warning sign of a leader being promoted beyond their potential.

## Individual coaching tips

- **Take in the richness of each role.** Don't neglect the finer details and nuance of a role. While you will be rewarded based on how well you have delivered in role, try to experience the elements of the role that are not strictly necessary for you to achieve your targets. Fully immerse yourself in the culture of the host country of your international placement or get to know the wider stakeholder group of your project instead of focusing only on key decision-makers.

- **Pay attention to your people-management skills.** While your boss may spend a great deal of time focusing on the business results that you must achieve in your new role, be mindful of the impact you are having on the people around you. Even if your boss never explicitly mentions the importance of people management, you are unlikely to become an effective leader unless you have learned how to harness the trust, commitment and energy of those around you.

- **Mindfulness and resilience.** As an accelerated leader you may benefit from learning techniques that will equip you with the ability to withstand higher levels of stress and demands. While rarely found in leadership competency models, techniques such as mindfulness, meditation and ensuring that you have several coping resources such as strong relationships, a clear life purpose, exercise and time out, will pay off.

- **Build in rest periods.** You are the best person to understand when you need to take a breather, recharge batteries and take a step back to make sense of all the experiences you have just been through. Not every organization may have rules or guidance in place to ensure that you are not overstretched. Unless you let them know that you need dwell time, they may assume that you can keep going. It is ultimately your responsibility to manage your energy levels and shield yourself from burnout. While it may take a little bit longer to get to the top of the organization, taking a less demanding role to consolidate learning and recharge batteries may be an accelerator in the long run as it may help you to avoid burnout or derailment due to incomplete learning.

## Notes

**1** Haag, R and Möller, H (2016) Internale und externale Entgleisungen: ein Derailmentmodell (German), *Organizationsberatung, Supervision, Coaching*, **23**, p 119

**2** Wichert, I (2002) Job insecurity and work intensification: The effects on health and well-being, in B Burchell, D Ladipo and F Wilkinson (eds) *Job insecurity and work intensification*, pp 92–111

**3** Winnubst, JAM, Marcelissen, FHG and Kleber, RJ (1982) Effects of social support in the stressor-strain relationship: A Dutch sample, *Social Science & Medicine*, **16** (4), pp 475–82

**4** Winnubst, JAM, Marcelissen, FHG and Kleber, RJ (1982) Effects of social support in the stressor-strain relationship: A Dutch sample, *Social Science & Medicine*, **16** (4), pp 475–82

**5** Folkman, S, Lazarus, RS, Dunkel-Schetter, C, DeLongis, A and Gruen, RJ (1986) Dynamics of a stressful encounter: Cognitive appraisal, coping, and encounter outcomes, *Journal of Personality and Social Psychology*, **50** (5), 992–1003

**6** Nutt, PC (2002) *Why Decisions Fail*, Berrett-Koehler, San Francisco, CA

**7** Nutt, PC (2004) Expanding the search for alternatives during strategic decision-making, *Academy of Management Executive*, **18**, pp 13–28

**8** Cope, J (2011) *Journal of Business Venturing*, **26**, pp 604–23

**9** Shepherd, DA (2003) Learning from business failure: Propositions of grief recovery for the self-employed, *Academy of Management Review*, **28**, pp 318–28

**10** Shepherd, DA, Patzelt, H, Williams, TA and Warnecke, D (2014) How does project termination impact project team members? Rapid termination, 'Creeping Death', and learning from failure, *Journal of Management Studies*, **51** (4) June 2014

**11** McCall, MW, Lombardo, MM and Morrison, AM (1988) *The Lessons of Experience: How successful executives develop on the job*, Free Press, New York

# Successful risk-taking

## 06

## Courageous people decisions in a risk-averse world

*There isn't any one thing that will stop someone from failing. Until you see a person perform in role, you can never be 100 per cent certain that they will do well. Derailment will happen from time to time and as business leaders we must bear the responsibility and intervene early enough so we can save the person and place them in a different role.*

BRENDAN TOOMEY, VICE PRESIDENT,
HUMAN RESOURCES ASIA PACIFIC, HILTON

*We need to develop people; leadership doesn't happen by accident. People need to be able to take risks and be rewarded for doing so.*

DR SIOBHAN MARTIN, EXECUTIVE
DIRECTOR UK HR, MERCER

## Taking risks in a risk-averse world

In this chapter we will explore how organizations can get comfortable with taking calculated risks on emerging leaders by posting them into stretch roles or promoting them earlier to more senior roles for development purposes. Playing it safe is unlikely to provide organizations with the future crop of courageous leaders who are able to deal with the many challenges of the volatile and complex world that we learned about in Chapter 1. However, taking risks now for future benefit is not something that organizations tend to be very good at.

Two prominent sociologists, Ulrich Beck and Anthony Giddens, have argued that we live in a 'risk society' – that is, a society organized in response to risk. Many of these risks are human-made, such as ecological disasters and terrorism. [1,2] As a society, we have started to focus on the future and with it increasingly on safety and the avoidance of potential future catastrophes. Consequently, risk management has become central to our thinking.

In many areas of our lives we encounter regulations aimed at warding off danger and trying to guarantee quality outcomes. Watchdogs and ombudsmen are in place to protect us from the risk of malpractice and bad service. Organizations have many types of regulation in place, too, ranging from health & safety and discrimination regulation to financial reporting and data privacy regulations, to name but a few. While these regulations ensure a fairer outcome for everyone and safeguard that individuals and organizations are accountable for their actions, they can also foster an environment where making mistakes is generally seen as undesirable.

At an individual level, we also like to play it safe. Studies from behavioural economics and psychology have confirmed that we have a loss aversion, which means that we would rather avoid the danger of losing £10 than taking the opportunity to gain £10. Psychologists like Daniel Kahneman have shown that we perceive the loss of something twice as strongly as a gain of the equivalent magnitude. [3]

Furthermore, organizations tend to focus on short-term results. As a result, employees are incentivized to focus on short-term targets, too, and are less likely to want to try new things for fear of making mistakes and not meeting their quarterly targets. The price of failure can be significant and include the loss of bonuses and progression prospects.

However, it is mistakes we learn from. Organizations face the difficult task of minimizing business and reputational risk while at the same time providing an environment that is conducive to learning, experimentation, and in some cases, failing. Developing and learning new things fast is intrinsically linked with increased risks as accelerated development means, by its very nature, that people learn in big rather than small increments. With big increments in development, the gulf between what a high-potential individual already knows, and the skills and knowledge they still need to acquire, can be substantial. With these gaps in knowledge and skills can come risks, and the scope for things to go wrong is larger. These mistakes can cost an organization money or damage its relationship with customers. On an individual level, mistakes can damage personal relationship and ruin future promotion prospects.

Of course, there is also a substantial business risk in not developing an organization's future leadership pool. As we saw in Chapter 1, in a global survey of over 300 organizations, 85 per cent of senior HR professionals voiced their concerns about the current leadership capabilities of their leaders and agreed that leadership development acceleration was a top priority.[4] In the same study, only 40 per cent of responding organizations stated that their high-potential talent can meet future business needs. Relying on ill-equipped future leaders is a significant business risk. However, this is a more abstract and harder to quantify risk for many than the immediate risk of appointing a less experienced leader into a business-critical role next month. We are better at understanding the impact of a candidate who may not perform in the immediate future than the impact of a lack of capable leaders in the future. When we turn this situation around and look at it from what benefits senior decision-makers are gaining, then we come across another interesting phenomenon – 'hyperbolic discounting'.[5] Research has shown that we tend to favour immediate benefits over future benefits. As a result, the immediate benefit of having a safe pair of hands appointed to a role is likely to outweigh the benefits of having a pool of well-rounded leaders in the future.

As a result, there is an ongoing tension in many organizations between filling stretch roles with emerging leaders for development purposes versus filling these roles with experienced candidates to guarantee business results. Several of the HR leaders whom I interviewed talked about the continued and frequently tough conversations that they need to have to convince business leaders to appoint high-potential candidates to vacant roles or important new projects. Organizations and business leaders prefer performance to potential. A common push-back that HR professionals must deal with is the request to give the high-potential person another year in their current role before promoting them or assigning them to a stretch assignment.

And it's not only top managers who are reluctant to appoint high-potential employees to important roles. At mid-management level, the pressure of delivering against short-term business targets can also be a blocker. As we will see in Chapter 8, not every manager understands the importance of making time to provide feedback and develop a high-potential employee.

# How to make calculated risk-taking work

There are three main factors that can help organizations reduce the inherent risks of accelerating an emerging leader's career progression. First, assign the right roles; second, ensure that the right candidate is chosen for leadership development acceleration; and third, put in place good processes and monitoring systems to make acceleration less risky, while still delivering accelerated development benefits.

## In practice: reducing the risks of accelerated leadership development

### Temporary assignments

We also offer short-term assignments, to broaden someone's horizon: different internal customers or different countries, but there are no financial advantages as a person officially stays in their old role. Rotations are only for three to six months. Sometimes we can arrange job swaps. People with a good level of experience can do these rotations. We don't want new starters as you need a good foundation.

Matthias Kempf, former Vice President Human Resources Emerging Markets, The adidas Group

### Checking for derailers

We help them get away from the obsession to get to the top to a more balanced path, which also helps to increase work–life balance. I worry about people who are too obsessive about being successful. We want people who have drive and are hungry to learn. We see who the hungry people are and who are the ones who want to be successful. We are better off working with those who are hungry to learn than with those who just want to be general manager.

Brendan Toomey, Vice President
Human Resources Asia Pacific, Hilton

### Using diagnostics

There is no such thing as normal development any more. It is all about accelerated development and on-the-job learning. Good diagnostics are important in this context. I am always sceptical about people's ability to assess leadership potential.

Dr Ursula Schütze-Kreilkamp, Head of Group
HR Development & Group Executives, Deutsche Bahn AG

### Starting early

The advantages of starting career management earlier are that you shift people's mindsets about what a career path looks like. You move them from a narrow to a holistic career management approach. You open their eyes earlier to what is possible. As a result, you get more rounded people and more rounded business leaders.

Paul Nixon, Global Talent & Inclusion Relationship
Manager (Europe, Australia & New Zealand), Mercer

### Incentivizing high-potential employees to take the initiative

People in their late twenties and early thirties are the talent we must talk about, but often can't as there are too many of them. The most promising of these people become active themselves and say, 'We have a great idea and we are approaching the CEO with it'. They are proactive and are being noticed. HR cannot do this on behalf of everyone.

Alexandra Aubart, Director Organizational
Development, LSG Lufthansa Service Holding AG

## Assign the right roles

### Start small

When we put people into stretch roles, organizations are taking a risk. The candidate is unproven and has yet to learn the ropes of the new job. While the emerging leader is getting to grips with the new role, the risk of mistakes is increased. One way to reduce this risk is to assign the rising star to a role in a smaller and less prominent part of the business. This may mean sending them to an emerging market rather than the equivalent role in the organization's main market, or asking an emerging leader to manage a smaller store, hotel or business unit. This means that the job will be less complex and if mistakes are made, the impact is likely to be less significant than if the emerging leader had been asked to look after one of the organization's key business units. While the unit may be smaller and less complex, the rising star nevertheless gets the experience of leading a business unit, which provides exposure to all the important elements of a business leadership role. And importantly, they are able to do so significantly earlier in their career than if they had taken an equivalent role in a larger market. Once emerging leaders have successfully completed their first stretch assignment and have proven themselves, it will be easier to place them in a key market role where the impact of decisions is significantly bigger and where, as a result, the organization's appetite for risk-taking is lower.

Another way in which starting small can help an organization make accelerated leadership more manageable is to take only a small group of participants through acceleration to start with. This allows the organization to give these initial participants more attention and support. Starting small also enables an organization to choose a small number of people that they have already confirmed to be high-calibre candidates.

## Assign well-known roles and recognize warning signs early

Roles that are well established and relatively stable lend themselves better to development purposes than newly created roles, or roles in new parts of a business that represent a big bet for the organization. The success criteria for well-established roles are well understood and it is therefore easier to spot if an emerging leader is starting to go off track. And if there are early warning signs of derailment, it is also going to be easier to fix the situation as it is more likely that there is a network of people who know what to do and who can help to get things back on track.

Some roles, however, even if well established, are less suitable for accelerated development placements. These are very specialist roles that require a lot of in-depth expertise that takes a long time to acquire. Equally, safety-related roles, such as roles in aviation safety or operational safety roles in a mine or on an oil rig, are less suitable for acceleration given the potential catastrophic consequences of an inexperienced job incumbent making mistakes in this environment.

## Make temporary assignments

Turning from managing risk from an organizational to a personal perspective, temporary assignments may be particularly helpful to encourage emerging leaders to try a new role. Where a high-potential employee is reluctant to leave their role for a completely new area, a temporary assignment may provide the opportunity to try something new as they are able to come back to their main role if things don't work out. While not as developmental as a two- or three-year role, it may be a great starting point for a person who wants to test the water first.

# *Choosing the 'right' people*

## Check for leadership potential

There is a long-standing debate about what exactly leadership potential is. What are the predispositions and characteristics that lead to effective leadership behaviours? Despite the accepted importance of the concept of potential, it is not unusual for organizations to assess an emerging leader's potential by assessing them against a long list of leadership competencies, which are the behaviours that we expect successful senior leaders to display. As McCall (1993) points out, the premise of leadership development should be that talented younger employees will learn from experience and change in the process of it.[6] It may therefore not be reasonable to expect all the attributes of a senior leader to be in place, even if only at a basic level, at a younger age.

Based on an extensive literature review and working with senior HR leaders, Dries and Pepermans developed a four-quadrant model of potential that includes the following categories:[7]

- analytical skills;
- learning agility;
- drive;
- emergent leadership.

A closer look at the model, however, shows that it still includes many of the behaviours that we tend to see in leadership competency models: communicating, influencing, strategic thinking, problem-solving, risk-taking, decision-making, customer focus, results-orientation, learning agility, developing self, dealing with pressure and setbacks, etc. This demonstrates how challenging it is to identify a manageable number of core attributes that help predict potential to do well at more senior levels. Also, as we will see shortly, each leadership transition brings new challenges and requires a new set of distinctive capabilities while past strengths become less important, in some cases even a hindrance. This further highlights the challenges of identifying what constitutes potential and at the same time points to the need for a more flexible approach to defining this concept.

McCall (1993) suggested that, fundamentally, there are eight elements that indicate potential, where he defines potential as 'the ability to take advantage of experiences that will be offered' (p 1).[8] As can be seen in Figure 6.1 these elements are centred on three main ideas:

- a willingness to experience new situations and challenges even if this involves the risk of failure;
- a commitment to learn from these experiences and to gather information, contacts and feedback to maximize this learning process;
- actively applying the learning as demonstrated through continued personal growth as a leader.

This definition of potential maps perfectly onto the building blocks of accelerated leadership development: the importance of learning from experience and being prepared to take risks with it; and the commitment to reflect on new experiences to extract maximum learning.

**Figure 6.1**    Leadership potential, McCall (1993)

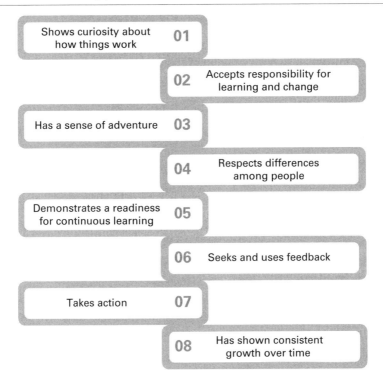

If we accept this definition of potential, then on-the-job learning and reflection do not only allow a future leader to continually grow but they also provide HR and business leaders a front-row seat for observing their talent in action. Using stretch assignments from an early point in someone's career enables decision-makers to establish if an employee has the underlying hunger to try new things and to actively learn from them. This attitude will provide a strong foundation for any future development.

## Check for potential derailers

It is not only a matter of ensuring that emerging leaders have the potential to go to the next step. We must also ensure that we understand their current behavioural strengths and weaknesses. The following behaviours have been identified as reasons for derailment where a high-potential employee is fired or hasn't reached their predicted potential:[9, 10]

- lack of self-awareness and resistance to feedback;
- being cold, aloof and insensitive and having trouble relating to other people;

- difficulties leading a team, including handling conflict;
- difficulties adapting own style – either with regards to a new boss or the requirements of a new role or a new team;
- difficulties achieving business results – driven by being more focused on career progression rather than delivering results;
- having narrow functional orientation, which means that managing outside one's area of expertise becomes challenging.

If feedback repeatedly highlights weaknesses in these areas, especially a lack of people skills and delivering results, then an emerging leader may need time to consolidate their learning and focus on developing these skills before they are asked to take on another stretch assignment. Furthermore, in the case of missing self-awareness of one's strengths and development areas, ongoing feedback is essential. We will explore the importance of reflection and feedback in Chapters 7 and 8. Emerging leaders must understand that being placed on an accelerated leadership track does not mean that they are infallible. Instead, organizations must help them understand that accelerated progression can only happen with a readiness to learn on a daily basis. This not only includes learning about new business areas and technologies but importantly, learning about themselves and their impact on other people.

## Assessing potential versus performance

Many organizations use psychometric assessments to test for underlying potential. Psychometric assessments are standardized tests that assess a candidate's cognitive ability, personality and motivation. Rigorous assessment can help to differentiate between those whose current performance is high but who are unlikely to be able to take on more challenging roles, and those whose performance is high and who also have the potential to progress further. We have already mentioned the role of psychometric profiling and assessments in Chapter 4 where we saw that they feature extensively in assessment processes for formal acceleration programmes. Personality tests, and in particular cognitive ability tests, have been shown to be good predictors of future job performance.[11] Some organizations supplement psychometric testing with data from assessment centres where candidates go through a series of simulated exercises, such as role plays or presentation exercises. Research has shown that assessment centre ratings account for between 8 and 13 per cent of future job performance in managerial roles.[12, 13] This means that up to 13 per cent of the variation in a person's job performance as a manager can be explained by their performance at the assessment centre. As a result, participants who do better at the assessment centre are more likely to do better in the job. For assessment centre data to be predictive of future job performance, the exercises that are used must be carefully matched to assess the core capabilities for the future role.

It is important, however, to recognize the limits of profiling. Several organizations have learned that trying to predict senior management potential for someone in their early to mid-twenties is often not reliable. A lack of experience and confidence shortly after completing a graduate programme may not provide a strong enough foundation to confidently predict if someone can successfully go all the way to senior management level. Assessments of an individual's potential may only prove accurate for the next one or two roles. To avoid longer-term disappointment caused by the recognition that the leader can go no further, and to avoid burnout or business mistakes, periodic reassessment of potential is important.

There are significant transition points that a high-potential individual must overcome. Charan, Drotter and Noel (2001) argue that there are a series of identifiable transition points in a leader's journey, such as from managing self to managing others to then becoming a manager of managers.[14] From there an emerging leader moves to functional, then business and finally enterprise leadership roles. Each of these transitions brings a change in focus and orientation. Talents and skills that may have propelled a high-potential individual earlier on in their career may no longer be enough to take them to the next stage of their career. More problematically, these early star quality behaviours may even become a liability. Charan and colleagues identified two transition points as particularly troublesome. The first transition is from individual contributor to manager of others, which requires letting go of being a good individual contributor to delivering results through others. The second troublesome transition point is from functional leader to business leader where an individual must leave the comfort of 'their' function and start addressing issues across functions, ensuring that all are balanced and equally attended to. They must understand the contributions of the different functions and move from a transactional to a more strategic leadership style. Interestingly, these two troublesome transition points map onto the two main career points at which organizations tend to broaden out emerging leaders' experience base: early career and mid-management level.

Given the potential difficulties that these two transition points can present, careful assessments of the potential to be successful at the next level are important. In the case of moving from an individual contributor to becoming a manager of others, for example, the focus of the assessment should be on people skills such as team orientation, empathy and developing others.

## Start at a young age

Giving a high-potential employee the opportunity to broaden their experience early brings several benefits. First, it allows a high-potential employee to try their hand at a new challenge without the risk of any potential derailment causing significant harm to either the individual or the organization, as the roles they are likely to take up at this earlier career stage will be more contained.

Furthermore, this early experience will help them develop organization-wide thinking and contacts, along with learning how to flex their approach in new situations. These are all assets which will make it more likely that the emerging leader will do well later. As a result, the risks of taking on additional stretch roles at mid-management level are reduced, as the high-potential employee is not new to finding their way through a new, unfamiliar and probably challenging role. This reduces risk and gives business leaders greater confidence that a cross-functional or geographical move later will be successful. The longer a high-potential individual waits to gain breadth of experience and the more senior they are, the more difficult it will be to move to a new area, particularly if this move is from a functional to an operational role.

Finally, as we just saw, early exposure to stretch assignments allows senior leaders to check if a promising employee really has the necessary hunger to try new things and the willingness to actively learn from experiences. With these early insights into the underlying potential of a high-potential employee, decision-makers will be more likely to take a risk on this person when it comes to assigning high-stakes roles later.

## Incentivize, monitor and evaluate

Finding the right roles and suitable candidates for accelerated development is only the start. To ensure that accelerated development efforts are successful, organizations must continually incentivize both business leaders and high-potential employees to take risks with development opportunities. Furthermore, they must monitor the progress of emerging leaders once they are in role so that any early signs of derailment or development stagnation may be spotted. Organizations must also evaluate and reflect on the successes and failures of individual placements as well as the overall acceleration programme. Let's take a closer look at each of these steps.

### Educate and incentivize senior leaders

For acceleration to work, senior leaders must take a chance on emerging leaders and put them in a stretching role so that these emerging leaders can show what they are made of. Most of the senior leaders with whom I have worked, men and women alike, can identify one or more people who took a chance on them and gave them the opportunity to try their hand at a career-changing role.

Before we can effectively incentivize senior leaders to give developing leaders access to stretch roles, we must educate these senior leaders about the importance of acceleration and their pivotal role in the process. For business leaders to be brought on board, they need to understand that emerging leaders can and should be accelerated. Senior leaders may have to be helped to overcome an attitude of 'It took me 15 years to get to the top, the new generation of leaders cannot get there in 8 years'. Career success must be redefined from being about time served to being driven by experience. Leaders must understand that it no longer takes 20 or 25 years to get to the top of a large organization. If organizations want to hold on to their young talent, acceleration is essential. Furthermore, it is essential that senior leaders understand their full role in the acceleration process. And as we will see in Chapters 7 and 8, their role doesn't stop with taking a chance on a high-potential employee and appointing them to a high-stakes role. Instead, senior leaders must continue to support, coach and develop the emerging leader while they are getting to grips with their new role.

Where senior leaders have taken risks and appointed developing talent to stretch roles, it is important to share these courageous job appointments for everyone to see.

## Incentivize high-potential employees

Once we have given senior leaders the confidence to take a calculated risk on a high-potential employee, we must turn to high-potential employees themselves. They need encouragement to put themselves forward for stretch roles, thus creating a virtuous cycle. When we have emerging leaders who proactively ask for stretch roles, we further help senior leaders take a chance on a high-potential employee. To help emerging leaders take a risk with a challenging role in a new area, it is important that organizations provide an environment where failure is regarded as a learning experience rather than the end of a career. Without such support in place, emerging leaders are less likely to do something that is harder and riskier than the role they are currently in.

Creating the right culture means accepting that even with the best profiling and preparation in place, there cannot be a guarantee that someone will do well in a stretch role. In this situation, it pays to stay close to a person, allow them to 'have a go', but be ready to pull them back and accept that it may not have been the right person for the role or the right role for this person. In these situations, we should make time for a development conversation with the high-potential employee and offer coaching. Furthermore, the individual must be made to feel that they are able to ask for advice and feedback, and express any concerns about the role. A culture which, at its core, emphasizes mastery-focus and advocates a focus on learning and improving skills will incentivize the high-potential employee to take on challenging tasks. The process of learning itself must be valued.

## Monitor

Any process that involves an elevated level of risks demands close monitoring and additional support. We will explore the importance of support in greater detail in Chapter 8. Regular check-ins can double up as support as well as an early warning system. Conversations allow high-potential leaders to seek support and at the same time they allow a business or HR leader to get a sense for how things are going. These conversations must be based on trust and the emerging leader must know that there are viable alternatives to the accelerated track and, if they admit to problems in their current role, that this will not spell the end of their career.

## Evaluate assignments and increase return on failure

Julian Birkinshaw and Martine Haas propose a three-stage process for increasing a return on failure taken by organizations to increase their readiness to innovate and experiment with new ideas (see Figure 6.2).[15] While this framework is proposed in the context of intrapreneurship, a concept that we already came across in Chapter 3 as one of the key experiences for an emerging leader to gain, it is equally applicable to evaluating risk-taking in connection with accelerated leadership development, which can be regarded as a form of experimentation – an experimentation with putting unproven younger talent into stretch roles.

**Step 1: learn from every failure**   As we will see in the next chapter, it is tempting to move forward without reviewing a failed project as it's something we would rather forget. The same goes for failed stretch assignments. However, to make accelerated development as risk-free

**Figure 6.2**    Increasing return on failure, based on Birkinshaw and Haas (2016)

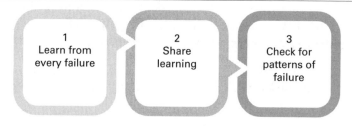

as possible, it is important to learn from each assignment, particularly from failed ones. Areas to explore are:

- the candidate;
- the role;
- available support;
- the process.

Table 6.1 sets out several questions that can be helpful to explore in more detail for each of these areas. These questions are also a useful checklist throughout the process to reduce the risk of failure. As we can see, for candidates we should focus on underlying potential and regularly check that learning is taking place. Roles should be in a sweet spot of being challenging but not too challenging and in an area that is business-critical, thus helping the person to gain visibility. Support should be provided from different sources. Processes must encourage rigorous selection, regular assessment of potential, ongoing self-reflection and check-ins.

**Step 2: share learning**    It is understandable that those involved in stretch assignments do not want to 'advertise' the failure of an emerging leader in a stretch role, as the failure reflects badly on those who appointed the high-potential employee to the role, too. However, if organizations want to accelerate their most able emerging leaders and develop a pool of future leaders who can run complex organizations in volatile markets, learning must be shared with colleagues across departments and countries. Hearing about

**Table 6.1**  Acceleration checklist

| Candidate | Stretch role | Support | Process |
|---|---|---|---|
| Does the candidate have potential or are they simply a good performer? | Does the role fill a blank space on the candidate's CV? | Does the emerging leader's line manager provide ongoing feedback and support? | Is a rigorous selection process in place? |
| Has the high-potential employee delivered in their last role or is ongoing ability to accelerate them further based on assumptions rather than concrete results? | Is the role stretching enough for the high-potential? | Does the emerging leader have an effective mentor and/or coach? | Is a detailed and recent assessment of the emerging leader's strengths and development needs available? |
| Does the high-potential employee have the opportunity to discuss whether they want a stretch role and acceleration to the next level? | Does the role contain too much stretch? Does it combine too many boundary-spanning moves, such as a promotion, a new function and a geographical relocation? | Does the emerging leader have access to nurturing and supportive relationships at work that help to bolster resilience? | Are regular reviews available to check for effective onboarding, progress in role and early danger signs of derailment? |
| Has the high-potential recently taken on other stretch assignments and should be given time for consolidation rather than more stretch? | Is it a new role, which makes it harder to spot early signs of derailment? | Does HR provide the necessary scaffolding (eg conversations, resources, training, contacts) to set the emerging leader up for success? | Is training on how to effectively use reflective learning in place? Are other processes in place to encourage the individual to reflect regularly? |

(*continued*)

**Table 6.1** (*Continued*)

| Candidate | Stretch role | Support | Process |
|---|---|---|---|
| Is the emerging leader resistant to learning from mistakes and taking on board feedback? Has their 'high-potential' label led to arrogance and an Icarus complex? | Is the role situated in an unproven market where clear success criteria and support systems are still missing? | Has the emerging leader been introduced to key contacts and decision-makers in the new area as part of the onboarding process? | Is there a process to take the emerging leader out of the role if early warning signs of potential derailment appear? |
| Is the high-potential employee's people-management skill development keeping track with the development of their business skills or is there a danger of one-sided development? | Is the role business-critical and does it provide visibility for the emerging leader? | Is the high-potential employee receiving practical support to get them up to speed in the role quickly, eg help with accommodation when in an international role? | Is 360-degree feedback in place to check the high-potential employee's impact on others? |

both success stories as well as derailments helps decision-makers get a better understanding for what works and what doesn't work. This in turn allows organizations to get a larger number of stakeholders comfortable with the idea of accelerating emerging leaders' careers. Regular talent reviews across the organization can be a powerful forum in which to share lessons learned with senior stakeholders, including senior management. These conversations should focus on working out every stakeholder's contribution to what went wrong, rather than attributing blame to one party.

**Step 3: check for patterns of failure**    The last step of the return-on-failure evaluation is an opportunity to zoom out and review all failures and successes holistically to establish overall patterns and any systemic issues. It is an opportunity to fine-tune the time–cost–quality–scope equation that we discussed in Chapter 2. To find a resource-efficient way of accelerating high-potential employees into well-rounded leaders, organizations benefit from reviewing processes on a regular basis. Furthermore, looking at big-picture data from across a business unit, or even the entire organization, means that a more balanced view of the successes and failures is available. This ensures that there isn't a particularly spectacular failure or success that unduly influences the organization's views on accelerated leadership development. When evaluating the potential cost of a failed assignment, such as:

- impaired health and well-being of the leader;
- reputation damage for the emerging leader;
- financial damage or lost customers;
- reputational damage for the organization

it is easy to see how organizations may steer away from further accelerated development efforts. Getting a balanced view of successes and failures and learning from each event is a crucial element of ensuring the longevity of any accelerated development programme.

## Summary

Accelerated leadership development is intrinsically linked to risk-taking. Taking a chance on an emerging leader and assigning them to significantly different or more senior stretch roles means a bigger gap between what the high-potential employee has been doing so far and what they are expected to do in the new role. With this increased gap in knowledge and skills, the risk of potential failure is increased, too. In a society that is focused on reducing risks through regulation, it is not surprising that senior business leaders prefer to assign a tried and tested person to a role rather than a developing leader. A focus on quarterly business results provides an additional incentive for assigning experienced leaders who are guaranteed to deliver outcomes to a role.

To get senior leaders' buy-in, we must first help remove attitudes that question whether acceleration can and should happen. Many senior leaders took significantly longer to reach the top than emerging leaders do today. Furthermore, senior leaders must understand their pivotal role in developing the next generation of leaders. The initial risk-taking must extend to supporting, coaching and developing the emerging leader once they are in role.

Organizations can reduce the risks associated with stretch assignments and accelerated development in several ways. First, the choice of roles can help to reduce risk. Choosing roles in smaller markets or well-known roles makes the assignment more manageable, early warning signs of derailment easier to spot and support more readily available. Choosing a smaller role can also lessen the impact of any potential mistakes that the high-potential employee may make while in the role.

Second, choosing candidates carefully will further reduce the risk. It is important that we select for future potential and not current or past performance and that the potential assessment is up to date and in relation to the next step that the emerging leader is taking. There are significant step changes in responsibility that the emerging leader has to master on the way to the top and a high-potential assessment in a person's 20s is unlikely to be able to predict potential for more than a couple of roles. Organizations must also make sure that emerging leaders are aware of their development areas to ensure that no blind spots and potential derailers are developing. Failure to learn from feedback, to adapt to new situations or to build effective relationships and teams are among the top derailers.

Once senior leaders' buy-in has been gained, the right roles have been secured and the right candidates chosen, it is important to monitor how candidates settle into their new roles and to have regular check-ins for potential derailment. These check-ins are going to be most effective if emerging leaders are assured that admitting to problems in the role or a desire to leave the role, or even the accelerated track, will not end their career.

Rigorous evaluation of successful and unsuccessful stretch assignments and acceleration efforts must be in place and shared widely to ensure that the organization can apply changes to processes and systems. Without such evaluation in place, the organization is less likely to improve their time–cost–quality equation. Aggregating findings across business units will help to spot trends and patterns and ensure that individual cases of derailment do not jeopardize the longevity of an organization's acceleration programme.

## Organizational design tips

- **Educate and incentivize senior leaders to take risks.** Putting a high-potential employee into a stretch role creates organizational risks. Educate your senior stakeholders that it no longer takes 20 years for talented employees to reach the top. Acceleration is possible and necessary. Incentivize senior leaders to take risks by educating them about the business case for accelerated development in your organization and increase their readiness to embrace accelerated development by giving them a front-row seat during early stretch assignments so they can see younger talent in action and get comfortable with their potential.

- **Establish measures of potential carefully.** Ensure that all assessments of potential include measures of openness to new experience, risk-taking, and a readiness to learn from mistakes. Ensure that measures of potential are not confused with measures of performance.

- **Profile repeatedly.** Check that assessments of potential are up to date. Assessments of potential are only accurate for one or two roles out. At each important transition point, take into consideration the specific challenges that an emerging leader is likely to face. Adapt measures of potential accordingly to reflect the key drivers of success at the next level of the leadership pipeline, be that managing a team of people or managing an entire business unit.

- **Choose the right roles.** Spend some time evaluating the suitability of various roles, markets or business units for stretch assignments. The ideal role will be business-critical, provide visibility and challenge for the high-potential while at the same time being a well-known role where early signs of derailment can be spotted relatively easily.

- **Monitor.** Put in place regular checkpoints to touch base with emerging leaders in stretch roles. Be aware of early signs of derailment and monitor for those. Have additional support ready to help the struggling high-potential employee and have a clearly defined point when a high-potential will be taken out of a role to avoid significant personal or business damage.

- **Evaluate and measure impact.** Build evaluation into your accelerated development programme from the start and ensure that you can have the systems in place to collect meaningful data about successes, failures and trends. Use succession planning forums to discuss these findings on a regular basis.

## Individual coaching tips

- **Help others take a risk on you.** Conduct due diligence on a role to assess whether it is a good development opportunity for you. If it is, help others take a risk on you by demonstrating your willingness to give new challenges a go. Say 'yes'.

- **Guard against derailers.** Be careful not to prioritize speed of progression over developing into a well-rounded leader. Avoid future derailers by ensuring that you focus on delivering results and that you learn how to build productive relationships with others.

- **Look for early stretch assignments.** The earlier you start looking for additional experiences outside of your area of technical specialization, the better. If you can prove that you can transfer your skills to new areas, then you are more likely to be given the opportunity to try your hand at something new. An early track record of being able to move to a different area will make you a less risky appointment.

- **Demonstrate potential.** Demonstrate your hunger for learning and a readiness to learn from feedback and setbacks. Also, be clear about the challenges that each transition along the leadership pipeline brings and start looking for opportunities to practise these new skills early.

If you demonstrate these qualities in your day job, you are more likely to be considered for a stretch role.

# Notes

**1** Beck, U (1992) *Risk Society: Towards a new modernity*, Sage, London

**2** Giddens, A (1991) *The Consequences of Modernity*, Polity Press

**3** Kahneman, D and Tversky, A (1979) Prospect Theory: An analysis of decision under risk, Econometrica (pre-1986), Mar 1979; 47, 2; ABI/INFORM Global p 263

**4** Human Capital Institute (2014) *How to Accelerate Leadership Development*, in partnership with UNC Kenan-Flagler Business School

**5** Grüne-Yanoff, T (2015) Models of temporal discounting 1937–2000: An interdisciplinary exchange between economics and psychology, *Science in Context*, **28** (4), 675–713

**6** McCall, MW Jr (1993) *Identifying Leadership Potential in Future International Executives: Developing a concept*, CEO Publication, G 93-2 (222), Center for Effective Organizations – School of Business Administration, University of Southern California

**7** Dries, N and Pepermans, R (2012) How to identify leadership potential: Development and testing of a consensus model, *Human Resource Management*, **51**, pp 361–85

**8** McCall, MW Jr (1993) *Identifying Leadership Potential in Future International Executives: Developing a concept*, CEO Publication, G 93-2 (222), Center for Effective Organizations – School of Business Administration, University of Southern California

**9** Van Velsor, E and Leslie, JB (1995) Why executives derail: Perspectives across time and cultures, *The Academy of Management Executive* (1993–2005), **9** (4) (November), pp 62–72

**10** Gaddis, BH and Foster, JL (2015) Meta-analysis of dark side personality characteristics and critical work behaviors among leaders across the globe: Findings and implications for leadership development and executive coaching, *Applied Psychology: An International Review*, **64** (1), pp 25–54

**11** Schmitt, N (2014) Personality and cognitive ability as predictors of effective performance at work, *Annual Review of Organizational Psychology and Organizational Behavior*, **1**, pp 45–65

**12** Hermelin, E, Lievens, F and Robertson, IT (2007) The validity of assessment centres for the prediction of supervisory performance ratings: A meta-analysis, *International Journal of Selection and Assessment*, **15**, pp 405–11

**13** Gaugler, BB, Rosenthal, DB, Thornton, GC and Bentson, C (1987) Meta-analysis of assessment center validity, *Journal of Applied Psychology*, **72**, pp 493–511

**14** Charan, R, Drotter, S and Noel, J (2001) *The Leadership Pipeline: How to build the leadership-powered company*, Jossey-Bass, San Francisco, CA

**15** Birkinshaw, J and Haas, M (2016) Increase your return on failure, *Harvard Business Review*, May, available from https://hbr.org/2016/05/increase-your-return-on-failure

# Reflective learning

07

## Looking back to move forward

*Learning doesn't necessarily happen through every on-the-job experience. It is the process of reflection about that on-the-job experience that makes it a learning experience. Reflection is key to extracting learning.*

RAQUEL RUBIO HIGUERAS, GLOBAL LEADERSHIP
DEVELOPMENT DIRECTOR, IHG

*Individuals who are not reflective and don't question how to do things differently will get stuck in one place. We are rapidly changing, technology- and client-driven. Those who don't build in the time for reflection will be left behind as they are not adapting their approaches and processes. They don't proactively anticipate the market. They are forced to react. They are lagging behind the competition.*

LES MARSHALL, HEAD OF TALENT, NEX

## Taking a step back in a fast-paced world

Reflection may seem a paradoxical topic for a book that focuses on acceleration. Taking time out to review a recent experience is often perceived as an anomaly in our fast-paced world. It is, however, an important part of accelerating leadership development. As we will see in this chapter, at times we need to take a step back and slow down in order to speed up. There was consensus among the HR and business leaders that I interviewed that reflection is a vital part of accelerated development. In fact, it is seen by many as the most critical element of accelerated development as it allows a leader to extract learning from an experience, to consolidate their insights and get ready to move to the next challenge.[1]

It is not the experience itself but the sense-making and increased understanding that we are gaining about an experience through reflection that helps us develop. Reflection is a six-stage process that involves the steps set out in Figure 7.1.[2]

We already saw in Chapter 4 that reflection, or reflective observation, plays a part in the experiential learning process. In this chapter we will delve further into the process of reflection. Moon (2004) provides a helpful distinction between experiential learning and reflective learning. She describes them as two interlinked but also separate processes. Where experiential learning involves reflection in new or challenging situations, reflective learning may also be applied where no new experience is present. We will also benefit from reflecting on things we already know.[3]

Reflective learning has received a lot of attention in education and healthcare settings, but is equally powerful in fast-moving and volatile workplaces as it is a form of mental processing that is particularly useful for situations that are complex or ill-structured.[4] In these situations, where the solution is not immediately obvious, reflection allows us to further process knowledge that we already possess to

**Figure 7.1**    The six-step process of reflective learning, after Gibbs (1988)

**1** A short *description stage* which focuses on what happened during an event

**2** An *examination stage* that centres on the feelings that were experienced

**3** An evaluation stage that explores what worked well and what worked less well

**4** An *analysis and sense-making stage* to validate or adapt previously taken-for-granted assumptions and concepts that guide actions and decision-making

**5** A *drawing conclusions stage* about what else could have been done

**6** A *future actions stage* in case the situation arises again

help solve a problem at hand. It helps us gain clarity and informs our actions. It also allows us to learn from mistakes, increases self-awareness and helps develop a better understanding of the impact of our behaviour on others. Furthermore, reflection encourages us to question, validate or adapt our way of doing things in the light of the experiences that we have gained in a recent situation. As a result, we may adapt our actions in future situations. Furthermore, reflection helps us grow personally and professionally by helping us gain insights into our own strengths, weaknesses and learning processes.

In an interesting study, Di Stefano and co-workers examined the performance impact of time spent on gaining additional experience on a task versus spending the same amount of time on reflecting on the task. They ran their study in a call centre where new recruits spent two weeks on an 'on-the-job learning programme'. Participants who spent 15 minutes at the end of the day reflecting on their learning from the day reported significantly improved performance over those participants who continued answering further calls and gaining more experience for those 15 minutes.

In a follow-on study, the research team evaluated whether it is an increase in personal self-belief (an emotional mechanism) or an increase in the articulation and codification of experience (a cognitive mechanism) that explains the improvements in performance gained through reflection. When examined independently, both mechanisms seemed to play a role; however, when examined together, the cognitive mechanism of articulation and codification of experience emerged as the stronger pathway.

Finally, when participants were given the choice between reflecting and gaining more practical experience, they mostly chose the latter – gaining more practical experience. People seem to prefer doing over thinking. However, this approach has been shown to be the less effective way of improving our performance.[5]

# A trait of leaders

As we have already seen in Chapter 1, reflective learning is an important leadership trait. Emerging leaders, irrespective of whether they are aiming to become a technical guru, the head of a business function or a business leader, are likely to face volatility, complexity and ambiguity. To be effective in these situations, high-potential employees must be able to try new things, as established best practices are unlikely to exist. They must also be able to fail fast and learn fast. This learning must include learning about one's own mistakes and how to avoid these in future. A high-potential leader must also be able to extract maximum insights from each ambiguous and complex situation in order to establish how these insights can be applied in future situations.

Reflective leaders draw multiple benefits as they engage with the various stages of reflective learning. These benefits include increased emotional intelligence, a greater ability to make sense of situations and being prepared for unforeseen situations, as well as developing their most promising talent, all of which create a competitive advantage.

## Competitive advantage

Taking time to examine what worked well in a situation and what worked less well allows a leader to increase personal, team and business effectiveness, thus creating a competitive advantage. The danger of repeating similar mistakes in the future are reduced. Extending the process of personal reflection about lessons learned to include the team yields further benefits. Opening the conversation to show that a leader wants to learn *with* the team from past mistakes firmly positions this conversation as a collective fact-finding and sense-making exercise that will benefit everyone, rather than an exercise in attributing blame and identifying culprits. A trusting environment where everyone in the team can share their insights enables candid discussions. It also increases the likelihood of gaining the team's buy-in to necessary changes that have been identified through reflection. Collective reflection becomes even more powerful when external stakeholders such as clients are involved.

## Emotional intelligence

On a personal level, reflection can help a leader gain better insights into their own emotions. Analysing and making sense of the feelings that a leader experienced during an event are an important part of reflection. Emotional intelligence, or the ability to understand our own emotions, those of others and the impact of our behaviour on others' emotions, will be enhanced if we regularly take a moment to analyse how we felt throughout the situations that we encounter. As a result, leaders are more likely to be honest about their own feelings, calmer and less reactive. Furthermore, sharing personal feelings constructively will help high-potential employees encourage people to join them on the journey they have set out for the team. As we saw in Chapter 3, some of the most important leadership experiences that an emerging leader should try to get exposure to are change management, turnaround and start-up situations. All of these require strong influencing and people-management skills and are likely to involve a host of emotions due to the uncertainty that tends to accompany these situations.

## Questioning assumptions and seeing connections

The sense-making stage of reflection encourages leaders to extrapolate learning from an event and compare it to their existing values set, assumptions and theories about how the world works. This provides an emerging leader with an important opportunity to continually validate or adjust their thinking and beliefs. As a result, their leadership styles are likely to become more flexible, their views of the world more nuanced and their problem-solving approaches more holistic. We already explored the power of international job assignments in Chapter 3 as one of the leadership experiences that creates significant opportunities for personal development. Living and working abroad means that an emerging leader will continually come up against unfamiliar situations which, if the high-potential employee is open to learning from these new experiences, allow them to uncover their own assumptions and question strongly held beliefs. This creates powerful moments of development. Furthermore, spending time on making sense of an event allows a leader to delve deeper and make connections between seemingly disparate events and factors across different situations.

## Prepared for the future

Completing a reflection process by focusing on future actions, should similar situations arise again, means that high-potential employees are more likely to be better prepared for future events. Not only are they more likely to avoid the mistakes they have made in the past; they are also likely to be ready to draw on better solutions faster. Leaders who practise regular reflection are also likely to be able to deal more effectively with unforeseen events as they are likely to have drawn valuable insights from other events. Furthermore, regular practice will also mean that they are more likely to be able to stand back and reflect *in* the moment as an event unfolds, and as a result gain a deeper understanding of the current situation faster.

## A learning culture

Finally, leaders who reflect and who involve their teams in collective reflection act as powerful role models for reflection. This will increase the prospect of people in the team being able to try new things, fail and learn rapidly. Furthermore, these leaders are instilling a learning culture that values self-reflection and continuous self-improving, thus creating a pool of high-calibre leadership talent.

### In practice: reflection as an essential leadership trait

You make time to save time. ... We can accelerate leadership development by focusing on quality. By quality I mean mindfulness, being less reactive, less impulsive and more purposeful, to deep dive and sense. Using observation, analytics and sensing abilities for a temperature check. Be curious and share how things impacted you. You need to reflect effectively: 'What could I have done differently?' You need to be ready to take and receive feedback. You need reflection in and on action. You can learn critical reflection skills. You will not become a leader without the ability and willingness to reflect. You need reflection in action: you will always encounter the unforeseen and technical skills will not be enough in these situations.

Dr Fiona Bartels-Ellis OBE, Global Head of Equality, Diversity & Inclusion, British Council

To be successful you must be reflective. You cannot make the same mistakes again. All successful leaders constantly reflect about how they behave and interact. They always look for self-improvement and for business improvement. But they are also very supportive of the development of their team. There is a critical path of learning and growth.

> Brian Callaghan, Global Head of Leadership Development,
> Executive Resourcing & Corporate University, Global Steel &
> Mining Organization

Our most successful GMs help their people to go through reflective learning. Over a 12-month period they sit together to develop them. Our best leaders show the importance of learning and create time for emerging leaders to reflect. They coach their leadership team and set time lines for career conversations. Some say, 'I don't have time'. Emerging leaders who are left to their own devices don't learn so fast.

> Brendan Toomey, Vice President, Human Resources
> Asia Pacific, Hilton

I see that our successful leaders stand back and reflect. It is helpful to share best practice among peers. It is also helpful for us to reflect when we come together and to review what learnings there are from a situation and how can we do things better in future. And it is helpful to talk to clients and learn from their feedback and their reflections.

> Robert Baker, Senior Partner, Mercer

If you can reflect you can learn and take people on the journey. If you don't reflect you don't learn from a situation. Through reflective integration we are learning what to do again and what not to do. If a line manager is not honest then people are less willing to go on the journey. They need to understand: 'Where are we going? How will we approach it? What worked? What didn't work?' It's a collective effort, people know you want the best for everyone. It's not a lecturing environment. If managers are open and candid and ready to learn from what has gone wrong, then people are more receptive to implementing the learning.

> Jo Hindle, Head of HR Asset Services, EMEA, Cushman & Wakefield

# Types of reflection

There are various ways to reflect. While it is an activity of introspection it is not necessarily a solitary activity. In addition to reflecting on their own, high-potential employees may also benefit from reflecting with others. Each approach has its advantages and will be suitable for different people and different situations.

## *Personal reflection*

Reflecting on our own is reflection in its most traditional format. However, while a significant number of the interviewees recognized the value of reflection, when taken as an organizational practice, personal reflection seems to be a relatively rare occurrence. It seems to be taking place almost exclusively as part of development programmes where an emerging leader is encouraged to reflect to help identify their strengths, development needs and career aspirations. In these situations, reflection is sometimes a one-off activity that does not readily transfer back into an emerging leader's everyday working life. We will see shortly what organizations can do to help to increase personal reflection at work.

### Journals and learning logs

Taking time away from the hustle and bustle of the working day and writing down our thoughts in a journal or learning log is probably the image that comes to mind first when we think about reflection. Journals may be blank or structured with a set of key questions to help guide a novice user. Users may have been asked to complete a journal weekly, monthly or whenever an important event takes place. Furthermore, journals may be in paper format or a simple Word document. Alternatively, with the rise of apps, a user may use a reflection app to help them review a recent event. The medium (paper, electronic or app), as well as the format (structured or unstructured), of reflection should be driven by personal preferences and also by the user's level of competence.

## Other formats for personal reflection include the following

**Mental reflection** In some situations, it may be inconvenient to use a journal to record our reflections. Instead, with a rough idea of the areas to consider, a user may benefit from using time while driving in the car or walking to reflect on a recent event. Furthermore, experienced users of reflection may reflect on an event as it is taking place. This means stepping back as a conversation unfolds. Useful high-level frameworks for such reflection *in action*, include:[6]

- head (what role does reasoning play?);
- heart (what role do emotions play?);
- habit (what role do habits and long-established response patterns play?);
- think–feel–do.

**Portfolios** Portfolios are a collection of different documents, such as photos, reports or hand-written notes that help a user make sense of events around them.

**Conferences or self-help books** Attending conferences and seminars or reading self-development books can be another way to help a user make sense of past experiences. These sources of input can be an effective prompt for a high-potential employee to test their existing assumptions and beliefs.

## *Reflecting with others*

> Reflection can be done through self-reflection, but we are our own worst enemies and suffer from confirmation bias. We all benefit from coaches for reflection.
>
> David Clarke, Global Head of People Capability,
> Syngenta International

Reflecting on our own may not suit everyone's temperament. As a result, some organizations advocate reflective, or learning, conversations where two or more people come together to reflect on the learning from an event. While this approach might suit some people better, there is a danger that reflecting with peers can be too superficial and that the conversation focuses too much on the *what* and not enough on the *why*. For reflection to yield learning, we need to be ready to move past the surface level.[7] It is important to recognize that 'lessons learned' discussions, common to project or business reviews, are unlikely to provide the same benefits as in-depth reflection. The benefits of reflection, as opposed to a formal review, lie in deeper, self-critical reflection where we are ready to look at an event from multiple perspectives. This deep dive allows us to make sense of our own values and attitudes in relation to the new experience.[8] Such deeper reflection may only be possible if we trust the person or persons we are reflecting with as deep reflection involves questioning the beliefs and values that underpin the behaviours or actions we are reflecting on.[9] If this trust does not exist, we may censor ourselves for fear of appearing foolish or incompetent. Reflecting with others can, however, also have advantages and either take place in a one-to-one conversation or as a group.

## Reflecting one-to-one

Reflecting with another person can bring powerful benefits, particularly if the other person is experienced at reflection. Being asked probing questions can encourage us to take our initial self-reflection to the next level and help us to deepen our insights and sense-making. Furthermore, another person's perspective will help to challenge our assumptions.

## Reflecting as a group

Organizations are built around teamwork. It is a common set-up to solve problems or to get things done. If supported well, group reflections can yield important learning and insights. Examples of group reflections include the following.

**Action-learning sets** Action-learning sets are a problem-solving approach where a group of people learn, often with the help of an experienced facilitator, by working jointly on a project. By working with others on a practical problem, participants get the opportunity to hear and see others' approaches, receive feedback to their own ideas and get plenty of opportunities to validate their own thinking in the situation. The facilitator ensures that participants learn and develop individually and collectively.

**Collective inquiry** Other group-based approaches are based on collective inquiry and include examples such as Future Search and Conversational Learning, both of which we already talked about in Chapter 4. Another example is Human Inquiry, where learning, exploration and reflection focuses on topics specifically related to what it means to be human.

# Challenges with reflective learning

> At corporates we are not very good at freeing up time to do reflective learning. There is a sense of pride that I am in back-to-back meetings all day. We feel guilty when we have a gap in the calendar. A classic example is people sending e-mails at 10pm.
>
> Stephen Caulfield, Vice President Global Field Services &
> GM Dell Bratislava, Dell EMC Global Services

While learning and development experts agree that reflection is an essential part of effective learning, many HR experts also lament the fact that it is a skill that is not readily practised in busy organizations. There are three main barriers to making reflection a reality in organizations: time pressure, a lack of encouragement, and the challenge of getting people to learn how to reflect effectively.

Organizations are focused on meeting client needs and quarterly financial targets. This relentless focus on delivering results creates long working days and hectic schedules. We are too busy and have many more important things to attend to. We rarely get the encouragement we need to make time for reflection. Organizations value action to the extent that they enshrine it in definitions of competence, leadership or high performance. Competencies such as 'energy & drive' or 'action-orientation' can be readily found in many organizational competency models and while many also refer to 'learning' or 'self-development', few actively state the importance of taking time out and standing back in order to consolidate learning. With time scarce, the only way to encourage people to prioritize reflection is to convince them that it is beneficial for them and that it is encouraged by senior managers. This, however, is often not the case due to several reasons such as:

- A missing business case – the business benefits of taking time out for reflection would have to be demonstrated in terms of prevention of error or improvements in working with clients.

- The organization's 'personality' – a sales-driven organization with a lot of big, extroverted personalities makes it harder to sell the benefit of quiet time and reflection.

- Generational differences – senior leadership teams that come from a tradition of 'I am the leader, I know best' have a bigger learning curve to climb than younger leaders who are more open to feedback.

- A reluctance to admit to errors – while crisis situations can be a powerful point for reflection, a desire to focus on the positive and to fix the situation and then move on may mean that reflection and learning opportunities are missed.

# How to make reflection a success

As we have just seen, there are several barriers to implementing reflective learning as an organization-wide practice, ranging from time pressure and a lack of support from managers to the lack of value attributed to reflection more generally and a 'must know it all' leadership culture. To overcome these barriers, we need a multi-pronged strategy, starting with helping high-potential employees learn how to reflect effectively. Good HR processes, role models and a learning culture will further help to embed reflection as a practice.

## *Helping high-potential employees reflect*

Reflection is not an activity that may come naturally to everyone. Despite being high performers or high-potential employees, some people may take longer to grasp the concept. The main challenge with reflection is to get a learner to go beyond the descriptive level of reflection and to delve deeper to explore emotions, to use a recent experience to test one's assumptions and to abstract and generalize learning for future use.

Moon (2004) suggests a two-stage process to help learners master reflection. Stage 1 focuses on sharing the basic principles about reflection and Stage 2 focuses on helping a learner to take their reflection from a surface level to a deeper level.

In Stage 1, learners are introduced to the concept of reflection, explore examples of reflection, often in the form of reflective writing, and then explore these further through discussion. Helpful tools and resources for this first stage include among others:

- providing a set of questions to guide the learner through their first reflections;
- comparing and contrasting reflection with essay or report writing;
- sharing examples of effective and less effective reflective writing;
- arranging for group work or peer support where learners who still struggle can learn from others.

Stage 2 focuses on developing a learner's ability to reflect deeply. To write effective reflective accounts, a learner must understand the role of emotions, frames of reference and points of view. Line managers, mentors and HR practitioners can help their high-potential employees through any of these exercises:

- writing an account of a recent experience in the third person to learn how to step back from oneself in the situation;
- reviewing an event from different points of view, for instance different people present in a situation or different disciplines, eg psychology, history and arts;
- exploring the impact of emotions and moods on the reflection by revisiting a recent reflection after emotions have lessened;
- working with others for deeper reflection and being asked questions about their reflective writing for further clarification, eg 'what made you write this?', 'how did you feel in this moment?'

## Development programmes

As we saw earlier on, the most likely first encounter for a high-potential employee with reflection is a development programme or workshop. Introducing an emerging leader to the concept of reflective learning and providing opportunities for practice can build the foundation for further practice. It is important to teach the concept *and* to provide opportunities for application. There are several approaches that can help establish reflective learning as a regular activity beyond training courses. First, adding reflection to a longer training programme, as set out in the In Practice box below, helps high-potential leaders reflect on the application of newly learned content in the real world while still being part of a formal development programme. Guidance on how to use reflection tools, such as journals and providing a set of questions to help reflection, are important starting points. Once reflective learning techniques have been trialled and embedded outside of the classroom, it is also useful to have them incorporated into other HR practices such as performance reviews. The final step is to incorporate principles of reflection into wider business processes, such as mandatory project review processes.

---

### In practice: embedding reflection in development and business processes

We have built reflection into our annual feedback flow. We have frequent touchpoints and everybody has a logbook. There are prompts in the logbook; it focuses on changes. Everyone needs a logbook. You must complete at least one logbook per year, but you can also do one per month. Some people say that they don't need that much structure, while others say that they want more structure. We use corporate process as an enabler.

Jennifer Duvalier, Non-Executive Director, Mitie plc, Guardian Media Group plc, Royal College of Arts

You can get people to do things through the way we design our systems and processes. For example, 'you won't be allowed to bill your client unless you file your review', or 'I cannot give you the top performance rating unless you regularly review how projects have gone'. How you implement these systems depends on the culture. If it's a rule-based culture, then you develop a step-by-step process. If it is an encouragement culture, then you share stories of people who do this well. Lots of companies have feedback tools. That should be part of the process. You need a tool that allows you to give quick and easy feedback and to capture moments that matter. Lots of people managers forget to do this. If there is no regular feedback then you end up with the hated, annual performance review.

Dr Siobhan Martin, Executive Director UK HR, Mercer

We run a six-month development programme. Every month the cohorts come together and are taught about leadership. We give them nuggets of information and then they reflect on how they will apply them. It's then about what they are doing outside of the programme. They have a learning journal and checkpoints every month to ensure that they are doing it. The journal sets out questions and encourages them to have conversations with line managers. A manager is responsible for making sure that they are reflecting. There is a peer group reflection, too, where they can share their reflections, for example 'I found this difficult'. Also, we link it to a qualification. If they have completed their learning log, they get an NQual (the old NVQ).

HR Leaders, Global Organization

The health and safety culture at my previous company meant creating a safe culture in which to speak up. In meetings with more than three people, we always started with sharing health and safety concerns and with reflection. 'What happened', 'Why did it happen' and 'What can be done differently?' Top leaders were role modelling this behaviour. We need reflection connected to transparency: 'What do you think and what do you see?' It's the ability to have honest conversations, to discuss the positives and the negatives and to share your own doubts. Working in this way is an important characteristic of effective leaders.

Uxio Malvido, Head of Talent Acquisition, Engagement & Inclusion,<br>Lafarge Holcim

## Create the right culture and use role models

Reflection must have currency. It must be valued by the organization and be role modelled by senior leaders.

Jennifer Duvalier, Non-Executive Director, Mitie plc, Guardian Media Group plc, Royal College of Arts

While these HR practices provide the underpinning for a learning culture, they are not sufficient to guarantee a learning culture. For this to take place, an organization must provide role models who demonstrate the acceptability and even desirability of reflection as an activity to invest time in. This role modelling can take several different forms, such as a leader admitting that they do not know the answer to a question or demonstrating a desire to understand what went wrong in a situation. This behaviour may not come easy in organizations with hierarchical or traditional definitions of leadership where a leader is supposed to have all the answers.

An even more powerful way of role modelling the importance of reflection is to actively encourage direct reports to reflect themselves and to support them in this activity. This support can take different forms, either by spending time with the emerging leader to help them reflect through a dialogue or alternatively, data from engagement surveys or 360-degree feedback can be used as a powerful catalyst to encourage a high-potential employee to reflect more deeply on this feedback.

With role models we have another important cornerstone in place to make reflective learning an integral part of an organization's development approach. But it must go even further. The adoption of reflection must not rest on the role modelling of a few senior people in the organization. To fully embed reflection as an organizational practice, the organizational culture must allow us to trust that our insights from reflections are not held against us. We require a culture where we are able to be vulnerable. Many organizations, however, are not good at being vulnerable as it is often taken as a sign of weakness. Instead of identifying learning opportunities and areas for improvement, there can be a tendency to simply fix issues and then move on to the next project. The choice of language can help people embrace the need for continuous improvement and make it easier to admit that they still have development areas. Turning a 'not achieved' performance rating into a 'developing' rating can send an important message that it is acceptable to have areas we are not strong in yet.

During the interviews, I noticed a much greater organizational acceptance of reflection in companies with a strong health and safety focus, such as mining, oil & gas and steel. Having an incidence-reporting process and a general awareness of the cata- strophic consequences of mistakes seems to make these organizations more open to admitting to mistakes and reflecting on past events to learn from them. These observations are at this stage based on a rela- tively small sample. Nevertheless, it is an indication that the wider organizational culture may indeed play a role.

## Summary

Reflection involves an in-depth analysis of a recent event includ- ing our emotions during the situation, how it validated or led us to adapt our assumptions and beliefs, and what we may be able to do differently in future. Effective reflection means that we must move beyond a surface level of analysis and be ready to critically evaluate our behaviours, emotions and views of the world.

It is a trait of leaders and separates managers from leaders, but it is often anathema in a fast-paced world. Reflection helps those who regularly take time to review past events to gain a competitive advantage through greater emotional intelligence, being able to make sense of complex situations and being better prepared for unforeseen situations.

There are several formats for reflection, including reflecting on our own, often with a journal to capture our learning, or as part of reflective conversations with others. Coaches can also be useful as they can help ensure that a trusting, yet challenging coaching envi- ronment enables an individual to move a conversation beyond the surface level.

Reflection is not always easy to instil in businesses that face time pressures, value action and where short-term targets reign. A lack of support from senior leaders who may not value reflection or who may see the admission of mistakes as weaknesses in a 'leader knows it all' environment further exacerbates the situation.

To nevertheless embed reflective learning, a three-pronged approach is necessary: organizations must provide training for high-potential employees to learn how to reflect effectively. Providing additional help by supplementing learning journals with guided questions and offering active reflection alternatives, such as peer conversations or coaching conversations, ensures that people who are initially resistant to the idea may still embrace it as a useful learning tool. Furthermore, organizations must provide support structures that allow high-potential employees to take reflection beyond the classroom. Finally, role models as well as an organizational culture that is comfortable with embracing mistakes and seeing them as learning opportunities rather than weaknesses help to embed reflection as a regular practice. There are indications that organizations with a strong health and safety focus, such as mining, oil and gas and steel organizations, may have a benefit over other organizations as their focus on avoiding incidents with potentially catastrophic outcomes lead to a greater readiness to reflect on past events and to learn from them.

## Organizational design tips

- **Provide education and training.** Build training about reflection into leadership development courses and other training programmes. Focus on helping employees move from surface reflection to deep reflection where they learn to stand back, critically evaluate their own beliefs and values, or take multiple perspectives on a recent experience.

- **Provide tools and practical support.** Provide a range of tools for reflection, such as reflection journals that contain detailed questions to guide the novice reflector. A well-designed journal can teach a high-potential employee how to deepen their reflection and gain important insights and learning. Arrange for peer-learning groups and make 360-degree feedback available to all your accelerated leaders. While feedback is no replacement for in-depth reflection, it can help create an incentive to reflect more deeply.

- **Create pathways for ongoing practice.** Help employees engage in reflection on a regular basis by making it part of everyday processes, such as development conversations, performance and business reviews.

- **Use role models.** Encourage senior leaders who actively use reflection to share their experiences and talk about the benefits of reflective learning. Role models show employees that reflection has currency in the organization and that it is a valued activity.

## Individual coaching tips

- **Take the initiative.** Don't wait for the organization or your manager to encourage you to reflect on what you have learned during recent experiences. A desire to learn from past events marks out high-potential employees. They tend to reflect of their own accord as they have a desire to continually learn and improve themselves.

- **Make time and space.** Schedule in regular times to reflect, may that be on a specific morning, the commute home or at the weekend. Experiment with different times to find a slot that you are most likely to stick to. Try different formats to establish what works for you – online, offline, journalling or conversations with peers.

- **Feedback.** Challenge yourself to get feedback from others by talk it through with them. Ask those you don't tend to get on with so well for a different perspective. Use the feedback as a starting point for deeper reflection but do not confuse it with proper reflection.

- **Deep reflection.** Ensure you go beyond surface reflection by asking 'what' questions Take a step back and reflect more deeply. Don't fall prey to your own biases and instead critically evaluate what has happened and question the beliefs and values that underpinned the behaviours and actions you are reflecting on. When reflecting, you will benefit from taking multiple perspectives, looking at the possible views of others and considering these alternative points of view. For maximum benefit, go beyond the here and now and look at other events that are either directly or indirectly related and that may have influenced the experience you are reflecting on.

# Notes

1 Boyd, EM and Fales, AW (1983) Reflective learning: Key to learning from experience, *Journal of Humanistic Psychology*, **23** pp 99–117. Abstract available at https://doi.org/10.1177/0022167883232011

2 Gibbs, G (1988) *Learning by Doing: A guide to teaching and learning methods*, Further Education Unit, Oxford Polytechnic, Oxford

3 Moon, JA (2004) *A Handbook for Reflective and Experiential Learning: Theory and practice*, Routledge, Abingdon

4 Moon, JA (2004) *A Handbook for Reflective and Experiential Learning: Theory and practice*, Routledge, Abingdon

5 Di Stefano, G, Gino, F, Pisano, GP and Staats, BR (2014) Making experience count: The role of reflection in individual learning, Working Paper 14-093, Harvard Business School

6 Thompson, S and Thompson, N (2008) *The Critically Reflective Practitioner*, Palgrave Macmillan, Basingstoke

7 Moon, JA (2004) *A Handbook for Reflective and Experiential Learning: Theory and practice*, Routledge, Abingdon

8 Hatton and Smith (1995) as quoted in Moon, 2004

9 Moon, JA (2004) *A Handbook for Reflective and Experiential Learning: Theory and practice*, Routledge, Abingdon

# Supportive environments

08

## Essential safety nets

*Sometimes the only way to accelerate is jumping. But you need air cover. Jumping into a new role in your late 30s can be dangerous… you can fall flat on your face. Is there someone to pick you up if you fail? In mid-career you need good support. You are likely to have a mortgage and a family. And this middle piece is extending as children stay at home for longer. At a higher level you are more protected as there are fewer people who can do the job.*

MARY LAWRANCE, FOUNDER, CARIANCE
EXECUTIVE SEARCH & CONSULTING

*The single biggest factor of good development and learning support that I can give people as a manager is to help them become truly self-aware. That often happens later in life but if you can help people to get there sooner, that is a great bonus.*

STEPHEN CAULFIELD, VICE-PRESIDENT GLOBAL FIELD SERVICES &
GM DELL BRATISLAVA, DELL EMC GLOBAL SERVICES

## Social support

As we saw in Chapter 5, accelerated leadership development comes with several dangers, such as burnout, the risk of failure and incomplete learning. In this chapter, we will take a closer look at the role of providing a supportive environment for those on the fast track as a countermeasure to the dangers posed by accelerated development.

The research at the start of my career focused on work-related stress. I was particularly interested in the role of support that we receive from others and how it can help us deal with work-related stress, in this case work overload. Social support is a resource that is easy to access and unlike other protective factors such as personality; it is something we can influence and develop more easily. This makes social support an interesting area to explore as a potential means for stress prevention.

There are two proposed mechanisms for how social support helps individuals. First, social support is hypothesized to be beneficial to everyone, irrespective of their levels of stress. It is deemed to be generally positive and to boost a person's coping ability, irrespective of what situation they find themselves in. Support is therefore seen as an effective stress *prevention* tool. With social support in place, an individual will hit detrimental levels of stress later than a person who does not have access to social support. The second mechanism proposes that social support is particularly effective at high levels of stress. This second mechanism proposes that social support kicks in to protect, or buffer, an individual in times of high stress. This mechanism is sometimes referred to as the 'buffering effect'. It is therefore regarded as an effective stress *intervention* mechanism. Research results are mixed as to whether social support has the ability to buffer people's experience of high levels of stress or if it works as a general resilience booster, no matter what levels of stress an individual experiences.

My own findings from a UK-based sample of professionals and managers showed strong evidence that support generally lessens the impact of work-related stress, irrespective of the level of stress that participants reported in response to work overload. Those with higher levels of social support experienced fewer negative consequences of having too much to do at work. Work overload is also frequently a stressor for high-potential employees on the fast track. Even if social support does not have the ability to protect a high-potential employee from the impact of work-related stress, there is plenty of evidence that it can at least lessen the impact.

Support from others is hypothesized to work through one of three pathways:

1  to reduce the importance that we attach to a stressful situation;

2  to tranquillize the neuroendocrine system so that people become less reactive to the perceived stress;

3  to facilitate healthy behaviours, such as exercising or getting sufficient sleep.[1]

**Figure 8.1**    Four types of social support, based on House (1981)

| Appraisal support | Instrumental support |
|---|---|
| Feedback that allows a person to gain better self-insights | Practical help such as doing tasks for someone, financial help, material goods |
| **Informational support** | **Emotional support** |
| Useful information, suggestions, advice and access to the right people | Empathy, love and caring, trust, encouragement and acceptance |

In work on resilience, support and nurturing relationships at work are often mentioned as a key coping mechanism. Supportive relationships allow a person to talk about stressful events, receive empathy and have events put into perspective by others.

The four different types of support that are frequently discussed in relation to stressful events, as can be seen in Figure 8.1, are: approval, instrumental, informational and emotional support.[2] *Approval support* refers to receiving feedback that aids self-evaluation, whereas *instrumental support* refers to practical help. *Informational support* is about receiving important information and advice, and *emotional support* refers to expressions of empathy and caring. In my research, I found that in situations of work overload informational as well as instrumental support were particularly beneficial for well-being. Appraisal support proved beneficial for only some of the well-being measures, such as sleep and positive affect. A supervisor's emotional support provided slightly stronger effects, but co-worker support was also found to be helpful. We will explore all four types of support in this chapter.

## Feedback

If someone is resistant to feedback, it impacts the culture of the team or the entire business unit. It is therefore important to select highly reflective leaders through diagnostics.

Matthias Metzger, Global Head of Talent Management &
Organizational Development, Continental AG

Approval support, or the provision of feedback, is particularly powerful for helping emerging leaders develop faster. It is an important source of information that helps a person increase their self-awareness and understand their impact on others. Emerging leaders who get feedback are more likely to have greater self-awareness. Where this external reference point is not available, there may be a gulf between how emerging leaders see themselves and how others see them.

Despite the benefits of feedback, not many of the HR leaders whom I interviewed regard their organizations as having a true feedback culture. This is not surprising as giving negative feedback is not easy; it's an action that many shy away from for fear of conflict. Difficult conversations involve potentially tricky issues, such as threats to identity, blame, defensiveness and plenty of emotions.[3] As a result, it is often easier to sugar-coat negative feedback or to avoid giving it altogether. Feedback must also be provided in a timely manner for it to be useful, and there must be a recognition that it is intended for development purposes and that it will not be held against someone's performance record for the foreseeable future.

While feedback is an important element of an organization's learning culture, there is the danger that we ask for feedback from those people whom we like best and who are most like us, thus limiting the amount of insight we gain. And as we saw in the last chapter, while feedback is a good starting point to encourage an emerging leader to reflect, it cannot replace reflection. However, feedback is useful to help an emerging leader understand the impact of a potential lack of reflection and self-awareness on others.

## Instrumental support

To help ease the additional strain of starting a new role, practical support can make a big difference. Being new to an organization or a job with a significantly different remit to previous roles requires additional support to ensure that the newly appointed person can get up to speed fast. In some instances, this support will be individually tailored. In other situations, it will be programmatic and formalized. Many organizations have formal onboarding programmes, often lasting several months, for new external starters. These programmes introduce a new starter to an organization's processes, values and culture. For internal transfers, these onboarding programmes are often a lot less formal and rely on a mentoring or buddying system. We will talk more about the role of mentors shortly.

As we saw in Chapter 3, one critical job assignment that is among the most demanding is the international assignment, where a new job must be mastered in a completely different environment. Not only the job, but life outside of work requires adaptation. The support network that we had in place back home is no longer available, and access to support in the new country is initially limited if not completely absent. Practical help with relocating to the new country and settling in can significantly ease the burden on the high-potential employee. This can be as basic as help with flights, accommodation and schools for accompanying children. It may also include language and etiquette training, both for the accelerated high-potential employee as well as their family.[4]

In organizations with a strong leadership development culture, practical support is also provided for employees on an accelerated path. This support can range from providing access to courses in areas where the accelerated leader needs more support, to getting access to coaches and mentors.

## Informational support

Another important type of support that leaders on the fast track need access to is the right information, along with advice and guidance. This can be technical information linked to the new role that a high-potential employee has taken on or more general career advice. To get up to speed fast in the new role, high-potential employees need as much information and knowledge as quickly as possible. Or it can be personal career advice and guidance, which may be provided by mentors or line managers. This can include information about available roles, warnings about an impending reorganization or advice about unwritten rules of how to succeed in the organization. As the adage says, 'information is power'. To gain the fullest possible access to available information, a high-potential employee must build an extensive network of contacts.

### Emotional support and making time for development

So far, we have talked about three of the four types of social support that I set out at the start of the chapter: access to feedback (approval support), practical support, and access to important information and advice. One type of support is still outstanding: emotional support – the provision of caring, trust and empathy. While none of my conversations with senior HR and business leaders explicitly talked about the provision of emotional support as being an accelerator, the expression of trust and caring is often provided by trusted colleagues. As we saw at the start of this chapter, having nurturing relationships at work are an indirect source of career acceleration in that they can help increase an emerging leader's resilience and consequently decrease the risk of internal derailment through burnout.

While some managers may also be providing direct emotional support, the more likely way to show personal caring may be through making time for career and development conversations. We will learn more about the type of support that managers are ideally placed to provide in the next section.

## Sources of support

As can be seen in the In Practice box below, support can come from a number of different sources, such as mentors, sponsors, managers and a general network of contacts. We will look at each of these sources of support in turn.

---

### In practice: sources of support

At what point do managers want to give back to the organization and society? This is not an age thing. There is a balance of taking and thinking 'What's in it for me?' and giving back. It happens to everyone at some point. Those in the giving-back phase are great to work for. If your manager is not supportive, then you need to find a new manager or a new job.

Andy Doyle, former CHRO, Worldpay Group plc

I couldn't do what I do now without my McKinsey training; it really accelerated my career. It was intensive training and we got thrown in at the deep end. We had lots of opportunities. We also had the support to be successful. Managers had high expectations of everybody. We were trained with being future leaders in mind. High expectations were communicated to everyone, which meant that you believed that you can do it. Every Friday we had half a day of training and on every project our managers were measured by the professional development of the team. There was a strong feedback culture. We had two-way feedback every week. It was very honest and open feedback. We were given opportunities – for example, to go to meetings with senior clients and present from day one. I was working in a team with impressive people. I could copy them and learn from brilliant people. There were also lots of female senior leaders at McKinsey.

Sarah Chapman, CEO, Faro Energy

I don't know what support system these people have at home or what training they have done, but in most cases, they have sponsors who were able to give them roles and opportunities where they could demonstrate superior performance.

Michael Heil, Global Head of Talent Management, The Linde Group

When a person goes abroad, the individual has to face many challenges, ie new language, new culture, new peers to interact with. Sometimes it involves moving their family... People very often feel excluded in these situations and need resilience. You need a network of people who can help with the transition; people who can help you learn about new processes and tasks. It is part of the stretch.

Raquel Montejo, Assistant Director, Learning & Development, IATA

## Managers: a first point of contact

Acceleration demands that less experienced, high-potential talent is developed in a focused manner. This demands additional attention and support from managers. Not surprisingly, managers are an important source of support for a high-potential employee. Managers become powerful acceleration allies when they are ready to act as development supporters for their direct reports. The most effective managers regard development support for their team as part of their role. They take an interest in their team's development goals, make time for conversations and support their people using a coaching approach. As part of implementing an accelerated leadership development culture, it is vital that managers know how to provide effective development support and that they are trained in coaching techniques and giving constructive feedback. They also need to be aware of the organization's succession planning and learning and development processes.

The importance of making time for the team's development is a theme that continually emerged throughout my conversations. There seems to be a consensus, however, that not all managers have understood the importance of team development and are not spending enough time on it. Having a manager who is not making time to develop a high-potential employee is widely seen as a career blocker. This is not surprising. As we already saw in Chapter 2, organizations often rely on development conversations between managers and direct reports as their primary career management solution.

In some rare instances, line managers may even go further and actively block a rising star's progression. Line managers are human after all, and it is easy to see how a rising-star performer may be perceived as a personal threat by the line manager. Even when a manager is supportive of an emerging leader's progression, the practicalities of losing a top performer in the team, and possibly even a headcount that may not be replaced due to cost cutting initiatives, may make a manager more reluctant to put a high-potential employee forward for a new role. As a result, managers must be brought into development conversations with and about high-potential employees early.

Good line managers who make time for development conversations, feedback and coaching don't only help to address their high-potential employees' development needs; they also act as role models for these emerging leaders who are learning about the importance of being a people or coaching manager. As we saw in Chapter 5, there is a danger that emerging leaders miss out on developing good people-management skills, either due to a lack of understanding of why these may be important or due to a lack of time, with delivery of tasks often being prioritized over people skills. Having a people- and development-orientated line manager as a role model will therefore help mitigate this risk of incomplete development for the emerging leader. The most effective line managers go one step further. Not only do they make time for career development, but they also help their teams to actively reflect on experiences they are gaining in their current role. We already saw in Chapter 7 how important reflection is as a tool for accelerating development.

## Mentors and sponsors

> Mentoring and sponsorship have played a big role in my career. People have stuck their neck out for me and have taught me a huge amount. I became more confident in asking for sponsorship: 'Would you mind phoning that guy to tell him that I am a good fit for the role?'
>
> Rachel Gray, Sales Director, Experian plc

In my interviews, mentors were frequently mentioned as I explored the topic of support for high-potential employees on the fast track. There is a recognition that mentors, particularly if they are willing to advocate on behalf of the rising star and are prepared to provide access to job opportunities, can have a profound acceleration effect on the speed of career progression. Such proactive mentors are sometimes referred to as 'sponsors'.

The support that mentors provide differs significantly across organizations, ranging from providing opportunities to debrief events and providing career advice, to acting as a point of contact when an emerging leader has gone abroad to take up an international assignment.

Mentoring support is typically divided into psychosocial and career support.[5] Psychosocial forms of mentoring include:

- friendship – I can confide in this person;
- socializing – the person socializes with me;
- parenting – they are like a father/mother to me;
- role modelling – they are someone I identify with;
- counsel – they act as a sounding board;
- acceptance – they think highly of me.

Career mentoring on the other hand includes:

- sponsorship – they help me attain desirable positions;
- coaching – they provide me with advice on gaining recognition;
- protection – they shield me from those out to get me;
- challenge – they provide challenging assignments;
- exposure – they help me become more visible.

We know from a lot of research that it is the latter type of mentoring, career mentoring, that has a positive impact on careers. While psycho-social mentoring support tends to generate feel-good responses and helps to relieve work-related stress, it has no marked effect on career advancement. In a review of studies that had examined a range of predictors of job promotions, it was found that working hard and receiving sponsorship propelled a person forward the most.[6] To make mentoring a truly effective source of support for emerging leaders, organizations must invest in training both mentors and mentees, and highlight what type of support to provide and what to ask for.

Despite the potential benefits of the right type of mentoring for mentees, not all organizations have official mentoring programmes in place. And when organizations have a mentoring programme, in some cases it is a light-touch programme where it is up to the emerging leader to take the initiative to find a mentor. Where organizations put the onus on the employee to find a mentor, it may not be surprising that only a minority of employees have mentors.

In past research, I found that in a sample of 1,000 professional employees from global, UK-based organizations, only 17 per cent had mentors.[7] This shows that only a relatively small number of people – about one in six professional staff – have a mentor. If we rely on mentors to accelerate careers, we must ensure that those who want to develop further find it easy to get mentors. Interestingly though, informal mentoring relationships, for example where a high-potential employee has stayed in touch with a senior executive after the end of a project, seem to be generally more effective than mentoring relationships where mentor and mentee have been formally matched as part of an organizational mentoring programme. Informal mentoring relationships offer greater career benefits for the mentee.[8] This may reflect the fact that in informal mentoring relationships the mentor is more likely to act as a sponsor as they already know the mentee's work. Formal programmes, on the other hand, may increase the like-lihood of people going through the motions if they are not invested in the relationship. This emphasizes the importance of good match-ing as well as training mentors and mentees about what support to provide and ask for.

We must also ensure that mentoring is fairly distributed. We know from well-established research that employees with the highest-status mentors tend to fare better than those with lower-status mentors.[9] This is one of the reasons that mentoring for women, while frequently advocated as a solution to 'fix' women's reduced career progression opportunities, often generates disappointing results. Women tend to have lower-status mentors than their male counterparts. We also saw earlier that the type of mentoring that works best is where a mentor acts like a sponsor and advocates on behalf of the mentee. We are more likely to do this for people who are like us. We must guard against possible affinity biases where leaders are more likely and willing to invest in younger talent who are like them. With informal mentoring schemes it is harder to track who is properly supported by a mentor and who is failing to secure mentoring support. Leaving it up to the emerging leader to secure their own mentor may mean that under-represented talent may struggle to get a high-status mentor who is willing and able to open doors and make things happen.

For the most beneficial mentoring support, we must bring together the personal commitment to act as a sponsor that we frequently see in informal mentoring set-ups, with the mentor and mentee training and the monitoring of mentoring quantity and quality that formal programmes can offer. We will take another look at mentoring in the next chapter, where we will explore poten-tial gender-related bias that may make mentoring less effective for female talent.

## Peer learning: right by your side

Peer learning is another source of support for emerging leaders. It plays a central role in the action-learning approaches that we explored in Chapter 4 and on which many of the project-based acceleration programmes are based. A group of high-potential employees work together on a project that has been set by the organization and that is presented back to the top team. As part of these projects, high-potential employees learn to collaborate, draw on the ideas of others and have their own ideas and assumptions tested by the rest of the group. Action learning is most effective when supported by a trained facilitator who encourages the team to learn from each other and work toward a solution.[10]

Peer learning also increasingly plays a role in the social-learning solutions that some organizations have started to offer. In these situations, colleagues share thoughts and comments on e-learning programmes that they have completed, or they share learning from projects they are working on. Some organizations also use buddy systems to help new job incumbents get up to speed faster with a new business unit's or organization's processes, values and culture. Other such informal arrangement are personal advisory boards or personal boards of directors where employees assemble a group of friends or colleagues to act as a regular career sounding board. Peer learning is also beneficial when it involves a cross-generational element. In these situations, employees get a better understanding of other generations and how to work with them. And as we saw earlier on, supportive peer relationships that provide empathy and nurturing may help to increase an emerging leader's resilience at work.[11]

## HR: the scaffolding builders

HR has an important role to play in the high-potential employees' leadership development journey. They provide the 'scaffolding' for an emerging leader's development. The support that HR provides goes beyond setting up and running the acceleration programmes. Among other things, HR teams:

- provide access to training;
- ensure the emerging leader has regular check-ins;
- help to keep development plans up to date;
- help secure stretch assignments and coach senior leaders to keep an open mind;

- provide support when a high-potential employee is applying for a new role;
- secure coaches;
- facilitate finding mentors and sponsors;
- share information about available support and how to access it, such as the internal careers service or e-learning.

Given the HR-to-employee ratio in most organizations, it is not possible for the HR team to provide a tailor-made programme of support for all high-potential employees. Therefore, the overall approach tends to be hands-off, unless the high-potential employee is part of a formal acceleration programme that provides additional support as part of the programme. Emerging leaders must take the initiative to find out what support is available. As a result, providing information about available support is an important aspect of HR's role in making leadership development work. Every employee must be clear about how to access available leadership development resources in the organization. This information must not only be privy to those who are part of a formal acceleration programme or who have either a development-focused manager or a well-connected mentor. As we saw in Chapter 4, formal acceleration programmes only tend to be available to a small number of staff and most organizations expect their employees to take responsibility for their own careers. To enable employees to drive their own development, they must know about available self-service support, such as career maps, e-learning content, mentoring programmes and internal job boards.

Furthermore, HR leaders have an important role to play in convincing the organization to take calculated risks in assigning developing leaders to high-visibility roles. They must engage in ongoing negotiations with business leaders about holding roles open for promising talent as a development opportunity rather than assigning these roles to 'tried and tested' executives. At a more fundamental level, HR leaders must also convince the organization that it no longer takes 15 or 20 years to get to the top of an organization. In this context, they must gain line managers' and senior leaders' support in making time available to support accelerated leaders through ongoing feedback and development support.

## Personal networks

> Networking is really important. If you don't have a network, then you don't know what corners to look around.
>
> Rachel Gray, Sales Director, Experian plc

Personal networks, and access to the right contacts are powerful accelerators for careers. Knowing the right people allows us to have access to important information, knowledge and expertise, which may be vital when we need help in problematic situations. Building and maintaining networks is, however, a time-consuming activity and as we saw in Chapters 5 and 6, accelerated leaders may be at increased risk of not having the right networks in place, either because they haven't attached any value to developing such networks, or because they are abroad on a new assignment, or because they have been too busy delivering outstanding results in challenging roles. Access to networks is particularly important where someone has taken on a role in a different part of the organization. Facilitating introductions to the right people is a powerful way of helping newly appointed managers to succeed in their role. We already saw earlier in this chapter that networks can provide the high-potential employee with access to different types of important information, such as technical knowledge, organizational politics and career insights. There are other important benefits to be gained from knowing the 'right' people, such as:

- gaining access to organizational resources;
- getting things done by knowing the right experts and people in the organization;
- increasing an emerging leader's social standing and status in the organization by being connected with people in power;[12]
- gaining access to protection from political manoeuvring or in times when a person needs to be picked up after having been made redundant;
- personal sponsorship and faster career progression.

These benefits are not surprising, as knowing the 'right' people gives us social capital, which is at the centre of how organizations work.[13]

## Organizational support and learning culture

Organizations can provide support to emerging leaders in several ways. To start with, there is senior leaders' support for leadership development; an understanding that investment now is necessary to develop leadership talent for the future. With this support must come a clear focus on being a people-focused organization rather than a technical organization that predominantly values technical expertise and problem-solving. With this focus on people should come a willingness to ring-fence some roles for development purposes rather than insisting on appointing tried and tested people to the role.

In addition to placing value on good people-management skills and rewarding for it, organizations will also benefit from instilling a learning culture that values tackling challenging tasks, learning new skills and continuous self-improvement rather than absolute ability, ego and comparisons with others.[14] The former ethos is referred to as *mastery focus* and has been associated with numerous benefits as shown in Figure 8.2. A *performance-focused* learning approach has shown to yield less optimal outcomes.

While mastery and performance focus are individual-level learning and goal-attainment strategies, which are often drawn on in an

**Figure 8.2** Characteristics of mastery-focused and performance-focused learning

### Mastery focus

- Using more effective problem-solving strategies
- Open to accepting challenging tasks
- Demonstrating a stronger belief that success follows from one's effort
- Attaching importance to developing new skills
- Valuing the process of learning itself
- Increasing persistence and effort

### Performance focus

- Focusing on existing ability rather than developing or improving skills
- Attributing failure to lack of ability rather than lack of effort and persistence
- Concern with being judged as either able or not able by others
- Valuing ability and high outcomes over trying new things and tackling difficult challenges

**SOURCE** Based on Ames and Archer (1988)

educational setting, they also enable organizations to instil a learning culture. Mastery focus enshrines in its philosophy many of the elements that we have already encountered in this book. This becomes even clearer when we examine the various elements that are deemed to help implement a mastery-focused learning culture:[15]

- the use of pre-assessments to establish any urgent skills gaps;
- taking high-quality remedial action to ensure that no high-potential employee is at danger of being left with blind spots that may turn in to future derailers;
- monitoring learning progress on an ongoing basis through quizzes, performance ratings or 360-degree feedback;
- high-quality training using the 70:20:10 approach, adapting it to the context and the learner's past experiences;
- using additional corrective processes where learning has not taken place, such as through additional small group learning or working with mentors;
- additional enrichment activities to provide further stretch and personal challenges for continued learning.

Managers and mentors can further help embed a mastery-focused approach to development by sharing their own exploratory learning approaches or asking high-potential employees to explore different approaches to mastering a task.[16] A mastery-focused learning culture is also well-aligned with the accelerated leadership development ethos that emphasizes regularly tackling challenging goals and continuously learning new skills. At the same time, though, mastery-focused learning has the potential to come into conflict with the risk aversion of organizations, as we already saw in Chapter 6. Also, organizations are structured around quarterly reporting of performance and results, which is a representation of a performance-focused learning mindset. Organizations must therefore find ways of keeping performance and development conversations separate.

## Over-reliance on support

People on acceleration programmes tend to be high quality. They get coaching support, go through a portfolio of learning. They also have regular discussions with their peers to explore what they have learned from the opportunities they were exposed to and how they are going to use this learning. The question is: do these people coast if the spotlight is off them? Do they become reliant on all this support? Some may.

Gillian Smith, Deputy Director, Head of
Early Talent, Government Organization

Receiving support is positive. It bolsters us against the stresses and challenges we face every day as well as in times of hardship. As we saw in Chapter 5, when we are dealing with ambitious, high-potential employees who want to progress and when we move them from one stretch role to the next, we must be ready to provide additional support during transition periods. Most of the HR leaders I interviewed outlined how support is built into their acceleration projects through mentors, line managers, HR specialists and peer learning. There is one note of caution that was mentioned by a number of interviewees and should be briefly discussed here: the danger of participants on acceleration programmes becoming too reliant on this additional support. Some high-potential employees may have been accelerated beyond their level of potential and start relying on the additional support they are provided with as part of an acceleration programme to keep progressing. This does not mean that we should advocate a 'sink or swim' approach, but instead that we must carefully monitor how much support an emerging leader requires as they transition through different stretch assignments. These assessments are best made in open conversations with the high-potential employee, which brings us back to the importance of trusting relationships and having alternative career paths available, an important safety mechanism against burnout and derailment that we explored in Chapter 5.

## Summary

In this chapter we explored the importance of creating a supportive environment to help emerging leaders make the most of an accelerated development path. Four types of social support seem to play a critical role in providing support for emerging leaders: appraisal support, where we receive feedback about how we are doing; instrumental support, which refers to practical, hands-on support; informational support, where we receive access to information either directly or indirectly through the introduction to other people; and finally, emotional support, which refers to care, empathy and nurturing.

Not surprisingly, managers play a key role in providing a number of these sources of support, the most fundamental of which is making the time to engage with an emerging leader and their career: to find out what the rising star wants to achieve, where their strengths and development areas are and how these can be developed further. To do this, effective line managers adopt a coaching style, encourage a mastery-focused learning strategy and provide regular feedback. They also open doors and provide information about forthcoming opportunities. While doing all this, they also act as a role model for the emerging leader and help the high-potential employee learn about the power of investing in people's development first hand.

Mentors are another source of support who can provide feedback and open doors. They are likely to have a different network of contacts to a person's line manager and can therefore provide access to a different range of opportunities. The type of support that makes mentoring effective for career advancement is akin to being a sponsor: opening doors and advocating on behalf of the emerging leader. Softer, psychosocial support that focuses on emotional support and affiliation has not been directly linked to increased career progression. It does, however, have a positive impact on job satisfaction and helps the high-potential employee deal with stress and guard against burnout, which is an indirect accelerator. Peers who provide emotional support and nurturing relationships at work are another source of effective stress protection. Peers also provide opportunities for personal feedback as the emerging leaders work with others in a group to tackle strategic or challenging projects as part of their action-learning projects.

HR, on the other hand, provides a lot of practical support, such as providing access to resources, securing coaches and helping with development plans and applying for jobs. They are also powerful providers of important information – available roles, processes and who to talk to. They provide the scaffolding on which an emerging leader can build their career.

Finally, organizations and their leaders play a critical role in determining the overall learning culture of an organization and with it the likelihood that managers, mentors and sponsors, peers and HR will provide the support that we have talked about in this chapter. Organizations that value results over development are less likely to provide the resources and funds necessary for acceleration programmes. They are also unlikely to inspire managers to make time for development conversations and other senior leaders to act as mentors and sponsors.

## Organizational design tips

- **Incentivize managers to make time for development.** Incentivize managers to develop their teams. If a manager who focuses exclusively on achieving business goals is deemed to be as effective as the manager who also makes time to develop the next generation of leaders, people development will not become a valued activity. Use engagement survey data and 360-degree feedback data to measure managers on the extent and effectiveness of their people-development activities.

- **Train mentors and managers.** Make your managers and mentors as effective as possible by providing manager and mentor training. Help them understand how to support your top talent most effectively. As part of this training, ensure that you address the impact of unconscious bias and how it may impact their decisions of who they support and who they place in stretch roles. Mentors must also understand that some forms of mentoring support are more effective at improving someone's career prospects while other types of support help to increase satisfaction and reduce stress.

- **Establish a feedback culture and provide feedback tools.** Ensure that your rising-star performers have access to constructive feedback from multiple sources. Help everyone in the organization receive timely and constructive feedback through easy-to-use processes and tools.

- **Build face-to-face communities.** With a preponderance of e-learning, online communities and the intranets, it is easy to consider offline, face-to-face communities redundant. However, building personal relationships at work, both in one's work area and beyond, can bring many advantages and open access to different sources of social support. Review what offline communities you have in place and how many opportunities there are for different groups of people to meet in person.

- **Make it easy for your employees to find mentors.** Mentors can be an important source of support for emerging leaders. Make it as easy as possible for your rising stars to find a good mentor. Leaving it up to the individual will make it less likely that they will find a mentor, and further decrease the chances that it will be a good mentor.

## Individual coaching tips

- **Build a network of contacts.** Ensure that you make time to build a network of contacts. This may not always be easy given hectic days and pressing deadlines, but it will pay off in the medium and long term as your network will give you access to vital support, such as information, practical help, feedback and not forgetting emotional support when things may get tough.

- **Ask for the right type of mentor support.** Be clear about the benefits that different types of mentoring support provide. Debriefing difficult situations at work, affiliation and friendship are likely to increase your job satisfaction and may help you deal with stressful situations more effectively. To increase your chances of career advancement, ask for career-focused mentoring, such as opening doors to new opportunities and sponsorship.

- **Use different sources of support.** Don't expect your manager to help you with everything. Explore how other people, such as your HR business partner, a mentor or colleagues can help you gain access to the support you need. You may also be able to get valuable support from people outside of work who may be particularly useful at helping you put things into perspective.

- **Set up your personal advisory board.** Get together with trusted friends or peers on a regular basis to get support with your career management issues. Sharing concerns, debriefing on situations at work and getting feedback from others whom you trust will provide you with a regular opportunity to gain different types of support. A mutually supportive environment may allow you to discuss issues that you don't feel comfortable discussing in a more formal set-up at work.

# Notes

**1** House, JS (1981) *Work, Stress and Social Support*, Addison-Wesley Educational Publishers Inc (1739)

**2** House, JS (1981) *Work, Stress and Social Support*, Addison-Wesley Educational Publishers Inc (1739)

**3** Stone, D, Patton, B and Heen, S (1999) *Difficult Conversations: How to discuss what matters most*, Penguin, Harmondsworth

**4** Wilson, MS and Dalton, MA (1998) *International Success: Selecting, Developing and Supporting Expatriate Managers*, Center for Creative Leadership, Greenboro, NC

**5** Ragins, BR and McFarlin, DB (1990) Perceptions of mentor roles in cross-gender mentoring relationships, *Journal of Vocational Behavior*, 37, pp 321–39

**6** Ng, TWH, Eby, LT, Sorensen, KL and Feldman DC (2005) Predictors of objective and subjective career success: A meta-analysis, *Personnel Psychology*, 58 (2), pp 367–408

**7** Katie Jacobs' article in *HR Magazine* accessible at http://www.hrmagazine.co.uk/article-details/critical-job-assignments-and-networking-most-important-for-female-career-progression-kenexa-research-finds

**8** Ragins, BR and Cotton, JL (1999) Mentor Functions and Outcomes: A comparison of men and women in formal and informal mentoring relationships, *Journal of Applied Psychology*, 84 (4), pp 529–50

**9** Dougherty, TW, Dreher, GF, Arunachalam, V and Wilbanks, JE (2013) Mentor status, occupational context, and protégé career outcomes: Differential returns for males and females, *Journal of Vocational Behavior*, 83 (3), pp 514–27

**10** Lewis, LH and Williams, CJ (1994) *Experiential Learning: Past and Present*, Wiley, Chichester, UK

**11** Jackson D, Firtko A and Edenborough M (2007) Personal resilience as a strategy for surviving and thriving in the face of workplace adversity: a literature review, *Journal of Advanced Nursing*, 60 (1), pp 1–9

**12** Laia, G, Linb, N and Leunge, SY (1998) Network resources, contact resources and status attainment, *Social Networks*, 20, pp 159–78

**13** Cohen, DJ and Prusak, L (2001) *In Good Company: How social capital makes organizations work*, Harvard Business Review Press

**14** Ames, C and Archer, J (1988) Achievement goals in the classroom: Students' learning strategies and motivation processes, *Journal of Educational Psychology*, **80** (3), pp 260–67

**15** Guskey, TR (2010) Lessons of mastery learning: Interventions that work, *Educational* Leadership, **68**, pp 52–7

**16** Ames, C and Archer, J (1988) Achievement goals in the classroom: Students' learning strategies and motivation processes, *Journal of Educational Psychology*, **80** (3), pp 260–67

# Women's careers 09
## Keeping the pace

*Don't allow for unconscious bias when offering or not offering some-one a role. For example, a new mother who has just returned from maternity leave. We need to ask her and not make decisions on her behalf because we think she will not want the role.*

DR SIOBHAN MARTIN, EXECUTIVE DIRECTOR UK HR, MERCER

*There is clearly bias about who we consider for roles. The shock came when we looked at our talent review data and our succession pipeline and saw the lack, or the perceived lack, of female talent, which is clearly not correct.*

HR LEADER, GLOBAL ORGANIZATION

## Glass ceilings, labyrinths and glacial progress

In the last two chapters of this book we turn our attention to two employee groups for whom accelerated leadership development is particularly important. Women, who *need* accelerated leadership development, and millennials, who *want* accelerated development.

Our main concern with women's careers is their reduced progres-sion to senior roles. Across the leadership pipeline, women and men start off evenly split at graduate-entry level, with almost as many female graduates employed in high-skill jobs as men (49 per cent versus 53 per cent).[1] At middle-management level, only about 40 per cent of roles are taken by women.[2, 3, 4]

Women's careers, more often than men's careers, hit a dead end or a plateau, sometimes also referred to as the 'glass ceiling'. Women seem to hit this glass ceiling as they are trying to transition from middle to senior management roles. Only about 25 per cent of senior management roles worldwide are held by women. This percentage has only increased by 6 per cent in the last 13 years, representing glacial progress.[5] One third of businesses don't yet have any women in their senior management teams.[6] Only 27 of the US Fortune 500 companies have a female CEO.[7] Of the UK's FTSE 100 companies, only 6 have a female CEO[8] and only a measly 21 out of the STOXX 600 companies in Europe have a female CEO.[9]

While the term 'glass ceiling' is well established, eminent experts in this area argue that the metaphor is misleading. Professors Alice Eagly and Linda Carli talk about a 'labyrinth' instead. This metaphor emphasizes the fact that women get lost, or are held back, at every step of their career progression rather than being impeded only at the last step to senior management, as is indicated by the glass ceiling metaphor. Clearly there is a need to accelerate women's careers given the slow progress made so far with getting more women to the top.

## Bias, children and reduced working hours

Let's briefly look at a few of the barriers that hold women back. The two most impactful barriers are bias and childcare arrangements. Cultural beliefs determine what we think is 'natural' for women and men to do, and what roles both groups 'should' occupy in society. Despite decades of feminism, there is still a deeply held view that women are the main childcare providers. And while increasing numbers of women in many countries no longer stay at home to fulfil a full-time caring role, their larger burden of childcare is reflected in reduced working hours. Despite more involvement of fathers in child rearing, women still take on the bulk of this responsibility, and consequently often reduce their working hours while children are young. At the same time, fathers increase the hours that they spend at work. Furthermore, data shows that while men work longer hours when only time at work is counted, when both paid and unpaid working hours (eg childcare and housework) were counted, women often report working longer hours than men.[10, 11]

More and more, organizations are making structural changes to accommodate women's reduced working hours and offer flexible working. While this allows women to stay in the workplace, it also means that women are more likely to remain at a practitioner or lower management level rather than ascending the organizational hierarchy. Progressing to more senior roles on reduced hours is difficult as women's commitment to the job is questioned and colleagues who do not have similar constraints are able to travel and take on demanding, high-visibility and career-enhancing roles.

Another important barrier is bias. Bias can be subtle in that we may not even be aware of it. Nevertheless, it pervades everything from the way we see the world to how we make decisions. A particularly powerful brake to women's career progression is the 'think manager – think male' bias.[12] Women's supposed characteristics of being nurturing, compassionate and sensitive overlap little with definitions of leadership. Leadership is more closely aligned with men's supposed characteristics of being action-focused, assertive and competitive. There are large numbers of studies that show how pervasive the impact of this mismatch, also called 'role incongruity',[13] is between women's caring attributes and leaders' decisive and assertive characteristics. The more senior a woman gets, the bigger the mismatch between the way society expects a woman to act and the supposed characteristics of a leader, which have been shown to be more masculine.[14] A review of over 70 studies, all of which explored whether our definitions of leadership are masculine, feminine or androgynous (combining both masculine and feminine characteristics), showed clearly that stereotypes of leaders are still largely masculine. While there is some evidence that, over time, definitions of leadership have become more androgynous and now also include elements of femininity, such as warmth and empathy, leadership is still most strongly associated with masculine characteristics.[15] Furthermore, there is also evidence that men define leadership in more masculine terms than women. This is a concern given that many senior decision-makers are still male, which will influence their perception of an 'ideal' leadership candidate.

When we examine 360-degree data, there seems to be little difference in how women's and men's performance is evaluated by the organization, at least for roles up to middle management. We see these trends clearly across a significant number of academic studies as well as datasets on 360-degree feedback from different organizational sources.[16, 17, 18] In some cases, data even suggests that women are the better managers and that they score higher on important leadership qualities, which can be summarized as transformational leadership.

Worryingly though, while women may be deemed to be as equally high-performing as their male counterparts, they are not deemed to be as *promotable*. They are often judged to be less ready for promotion than men and when they are promoted, it happens in smaller increments or they are appointed to interim roles.[19] We will come back to this point shortly. Also, when it comes to senior leadership roles, we have already seen how a clash between supposed female characteristics and leadership characteristics put women at a disadvantage. These are substantial barriers for women to overcome.

## Senior women get there faster

Interestingly, women who get to the top of an organization seem to get there faster. Board data shows that female board directors are on average younger than their male counterparts.[20, 21] This may be because more women are still predominantly in functional areas, such as HR or finance, which allow for faster progression than general management roles. Another reason why the women who get to the top may get there faster is that those who are focused on getting to the top understand that getting to senior roles will be much harder with the additional commitments of a family. My work with organizations, as well as the research for my last book, shows that while it may be possible to do a senior role with some flexibility and possibly even on somewhat reduced hours, it is much harder to get to this level while working flexibly or reduced hours. The competition for top roles is tough and demands 100 per cent dedication. Furthermore, there is a financial benefit to getting to senior roles before starting a family as an increased salary allows for better childcare and additional help at home. Another reason why women may get to the top faster is that they need to be high flyers who are head and shoulders above their male colleagues to overcome the 'think manager – think male' bias to keep progressing. As a result, they deliver outstanding work and therefore receive acceleration at each stage. If women want to get all the way to the top, they need to do so on an accelerated track. It's the fast track or the glass ceiling.

## Women's career progression

Before we explore best practice of how to accelerate women's careers despite these additional hurdles, let us take a quick look at evidence from research into women's general career success. Are there any factors we need to pay particular attention to when it comes to accelerating women's careers, over and above the factors that we have already explored in this book? To recap, the main factors are:

- building a broad base of experiences through stretching job assignments;
- getting access to support systems;
- taking time to reflect;
- taking career risks with stretch assignments as an individual and with unproven high-potential employees as an organization.

My past research, while still at IBM's Smarter Workforce Institute, shows repeatedly that the three top drivers of women's career progression are, in order of importance:[22]

1 *Critical job assignments* (accounting for 26 per cent of the difference between being promoted and not promoted). We checked for a set of ten different critical job assignments, very similar in definition to the ones we have already encountered in Chapter 3. The more varied the assignments that a woman has had, the more likely she was to have been promoted in the last five years.

2 *Politically skilled networking* (17 per cent). This included attributes such as spending time to build and maintain networks as well as understanding power dynamics and being good at understanding personal motives and interests.

3 *Risk-embracing opportunity seeking* (17 per cent). Here we explored how much professionals were ready to take on risks, such as applying for new roles for which they didn't have all the requirements or that were outside of their comfort zone, as well as for people's initiative in finding new development opportunities.

These findings, based on samples of non-IBM respondents, were replicated across three different studies, covering five different countries (UK, US, Brazil, China and Japan).[23]

It is encouraging to see that the factors that are linked to women generally having better chances of gaining a promotion also play a role in accelerated development. This may not be surprising, as we saw that the women who do progress to the top often do so on the fast track. Worryingly though, while these factors are critical for women's careers, they are also less frequently reported by women. We will look at this in more detail as we go through each of the following enablers for women's career acceleration:

- Access to stretching job assignments to provide breadth of experience.

- Access to support, such as mentors and managers as well as more general access to senior networks, which include people who can provide access to roles. This also includes strong HR support that helps to tackle bias against women as leaders.

- Reflective learning (which must not turn into 'I am not ready yet and will therefore not put myself forward' hesitations).

- Being proactive in finding new opportunities and demonstrating a readiness to take on new roles.

# Making accelerated leadership development work for women

Women face additional barriers for each of the career accelerators we have just summarized: breadth of roles, support/networks, reflective learning and risk-taking (see Figure 9.1). We will take a closer look at each and examine possible solutions.

## Stretch roles and access to these roles

Career-enhancing stretch roles are one of the three core pillars of accelerated development. They are also the top driver of women's career progression. In three separate studies, we found that critical job assignments, or stretch roles, account for about a quarter of

**Figure 9.1** Accelerators and barriers to women's career progression

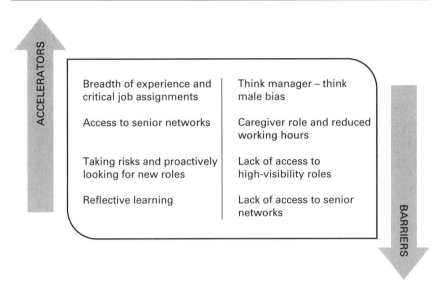

the difference for women between being promoted and not being promoted.[24] While having a breadth of roles on one's CV also plays a role for men's careers, my work showed that it wasn't as important a factor for men as for women. Men's careers also benefited from supervisor support (ie a manager who believed in them and actively supported their career progression) and access to objective HR processes. Women benefited much less from these and instead had to rely more on showing that they had already gained the right experience. The reason that critical job assignments are so important for women goes beyond the benefits of broadening one's experiences. It is also a vital tool to help women overcome the 'think manager – think male' bias that is often present in promotion decisions.

## Performance versus promotability

As we saw earlier on, when it comes to assessing men's and women's work-related performance there aren't any great differences. This applies for roles up to middle management. When it comes to giving someone a more senior role, there is another important dimension to consider in addition to performance: their promotability. This refers to their perceived readiness to take on a more senior role. While high performance may be a prerequisite for a promotion or an appointment to a stretch role, it is not sufficient. Recruiting managers want to ensure that the candidate in question is ready to take on the more demanding role. 'The 'think manager – think male' bias means that female candidates are often deemed to be less ready and promotable for more senior roles. They often constitute non-traditional hires, particularly so for roles in male-dominated areas, such as operational or senior roles, or international placements in patriarchal countries.

In a small-scale study into the selection decisions of senior leaders and the rationale for these decisions, it became clear that women are more likely to be selected for interim roles where they need to prove themselves before being assigned to the role permanently.[25] Where we have to make risky hiring decisions, which often means not knowing how someone will do in role, we are more likely to go back to gut instinct and who we know. This will favour male candidates and means that women are less likely to be given the benefit of the doubt. As a results, they are less likely to get the role.

Several HR leaders I talked to recognize this problem and have seen it play out in their organization's data. After rigorously evaluating potential and promotability ratings across the pipeline, it becomes apparent that women's potential seems to suddenly drop off after mid-management level. The changes in potential ratings between middle and senior management-level roles are so pronounced that they are likely to reflect bias rather than the clear majority of previously high-potential women suddenly becoming low potential.

## Difficulties in securing career-enhancing roles

In addition to bias, other reasons for women not gaining access to career-enhancing roles include not being visible in senior decision-making circles where roles are assigned and experiencing benign sexism, where women are not offered difficult roles due to a misguided desire to protect them from working in unpleasant environments.[26] Let's look at what this means in actual numbers.

In my study of 3,000 professional men and women from five countries, the most frequently reported assignments for men and women were working in a new functional area (67 and 68 per cent for women and men respectively), early stretch assignments (65 per cent for both women and men) and people management responsibility (62 and

66 per cent for women and men respectively). Around 60 per cent of men indicated that they also had experienced:

- an operational front-line role;
- a general management role;
- a start-up role where they had built something new, like a product, process or service.

Women start to report lower numbers for having experienced these roles with the gap ranging from 5 to 8 per cent.

Furthermore, about 50 per cent of men reported experience of:

- being a member of an executive team;
- large-scale change management projects;
- turnaround projects.

Again, fewer women had experienced these roles with the gaps between women and men ranging from 3 per cent for being a member of an executive team to 8 per cent for large-scale change management roles.[27]

The experience that was reported least frequently for both women and men, and that showed that biggest gender gap in experience, was the international assignment. While 45 per cent of men reported this experience, only 35 per cent of women reported it.

## International assignments

As we saw in Chapter 3, while there is not always agreement on what types of experience are important to accelerate an emerging leader's career, the clear majority of HR leaders who I talked to agreed that international experience was important. International experience is one of the types of experience that is particularly difficult for women to obtain and data shows that women are less likely than men to be posted on international assignments. This is driven by a number of organizational concerns. Organizations may feel reluctant. To send women to patriarchal societies where they may struggle to do well. Furthermore, transferring women with family and children is a cost-intensive undertaking and something that both the organizations and the woman herself may be hesitant to embrace. There is also often no help for an expat's partner to get a job. Several organizations have recognized that stipulating international experience as a prerequisite for senior roles disproportionally excludes women from the selection process. As a result, some organizations have dropped international experience from their requirements for promotion to senior roles.

## Ongoing dialogue, preparation and dwell time

We have already talked about the importance of ongoing development discussions to guard against high-potential employees' derailment in Chapter 5. These conversations are particularly important for women as they ensure that a woman is ready to move when an opportunity comes up. Where women have a partner or a family, they are less likely to be able to take on a role if it is sprung on them. They are likely to need more time to plan.

Furthermore, development conversations not only help women get the roles that help them to accelerate their careers, they also ensure that once on an accelerated track, they do not derail. As we saw in Chapter 5, dwell time, the opportunity to consolidate learning and take a step back to recharge batteries, is important for an accelerated leader to succeed. This applies to female talent, too. In some situations, while well intended, organizations may give women less dwell time in a desire to move more women to the top of an organization. As soon as a woman with potential is spotted she is put on the fast track. The unintended consequence of this can be that high-potential women derail or that they are more likely to lose their jobs in times of downsizing or restructuring as they have less broad or consolidated career histories than their male counterparts.

### In practice: additional hurdles for women's career acceleration

We often provide women with stretch assignments, but we don't provide them with the right contacts. We throw them into the role and hope they will cope. But often they don't. The right contacts are firstly at a technical level. We must help identify who are the right people to connect with to solve problems. And secondly, who are the right people at the plant, the right political contacts and the right sponsors. We must ensure that they don't make the wrong alliances. For women, it is really important to establish credibility in a male-dominated environment and to deal with push-back from the team. A sponsor is needed to manage this push-back. The sponsor makes it clear that the person is supported by the organization. Women need more support as they must establish their credibility in addition to everything else.

Uxio Malvido, Head of Talent Acquisition, Engagement & Inclusion, Lafarge Holcim

We had 40 women and 60 men on the accelerated programme. We had more women at manager level, but more men were nominated. The women went on the international assignments on their own and the men went with partners. The organization was happy to support partners going along. The partners of the men were happy to give up careers – none of the men on the programme left their partners behind. The women had married professional men and so the men couldn't go with them. All the women left their partners behind. As a result, the women weren't open to extending their stay; they wanted to get back. The men, however, were open to extending their stay. None of the women were or became mothers on the programme, but most of the men became fathers. It wasn't motherhood that derailed the women. Women found it very hard. The men moved to other more senior roles. The women all came back and got similar roles to the ones when they left. We only retained 40 per cent of these high-potential employees and we couldn't keep the females. The minute you label them, it creates expectations and we couldn't meet those expectations and they left. Men did better on the programme and were promoted faster. This was due to bias of senior leaders who were mostly men.

HR Leader, Global Organization

## Support

### Providing access to the right networks

To overcome the promotability barrier and get access to career-enabling projects, women need access to networks. For my last book, I conducted an in-depth study of just under 50 senior women and explored how these women had secured each of their career-enabling stretch assignments. Just under half of the roles were obtained by being approached by someone more senior, either in their current organization (36 per cent) or contacts outside the organization (10 per cent). The other half of the roles were accessed after a woman had asked her boss for a new challenge (17 per cent) or as part of going through a formal selection, head-hunting or project staffing process (37 per cent).[28] This shows just how important access to networks are, alongside pro-actively sharing their desire for a new role and taking the initiative, a characteristic we talked about in Chapters 4 and 6.

Having the right contacts continues to be important for women even after they have secured a stretch assignment. In addition to access to knowledge, which we explored in Chapter 8, there are additional types of support that are particularly important for women. First off, women need support with establishing credibility. Often, women must establish their credibility, particularly if they are new to an area or business unit. This is also the case if women are promoted to senior roles or traditionally masculine roles. Sponsors can help deal with push-back from a woman's new team and colleagues.

Furthermore, women need access to a safety net – group of people who look out for her and who are there to pick her up if a role goes badly or she derails. Men need the same support, and often find this support in the form of the so-called 'old boys' club'. For women, the equivalent 'old girls' club' may not yet be large enough or senior enough to provide the same level of support for women. This means that women also need access to the 'old boys' club', which may be harder for them to achieve as it is easier for senior men to sponsor and support younger men rather than younger women due to greater affinity and for fear of gossip.

**The queen bee syndrome**    Let me at this stage also share my concerns about the notion that more senior women pull up the drawbridge behind them and don't support more junior women, the so-called 'queen bee syndrome'. For me the queen bee syndrome has always been a reflection of gender stereotypes; we expect women to be nurturing and supportive and if they are not, they break gender norms. As a result, we evaluate their behaviour more harshly. Not all men nurture and support more junior men. If they don't, then we seem to accept this.

A large-scale, cross-cultural study that we ran at IBM's Smarter Workforce Institute, in collaboration with Dr Samantha Paustian Underdahl and her colleagues at Northwestern University, showed that in countries with higher levels of egalitarianism between the sexes, the queen bee syndrome was not evident.[29] It was only in patriarchal countries with lower gender egalitarianism or in organizations with a male CEO where the syndrome emerged. This points to context and culture as a driving force behind women's lack of support for younger talent. It is easy to see that in a culture where women are valued less, it is harder for women to bring other women up behind them. Furthermore, male-dominated environments may make women the harshest judges of other women as female scarcity at the top or in certain roles means that they are still regarded as 'the women' rather than just another job incumbent. In these situations, women may fear that bringing any other woman who is not outstanding into this circle may tarnish their own reputation as 'a woman'. Kanter suggested that it is only when women make up about 30 per cent of a group that they stop being 'the women' and simply become job incumbents. Furthermore, research on women on boards has shown that women's impact on boards seems to become positive as soon as a critical mass of three female board directors is achieved. Once this number is reached, women on boards have stopped being an anomaly. As a result, a woman's contribution is less likely to be a 'woman's' contribution and instead becomes just 'a' contribution.[30, 31, 32]

## Training mentors for better support

Mentoring is one of the sources of support that organizations put in place to help emerging leaders succeed on their accelerated journey. This is particularly the case for women. Even outside of accelerated leadership development, mentoring is often proposed as a way of helping fix the reduced progression opportunities for women. As we already saw in Chapter 8, mentors must be trained to understand what type of mentoring will most likely generate career benefits. There are added complexities when it comes to mentoring women. It has been shown that in situations in which both women and men have access to the mentoring, it is men who benefit more from these relationships. For men, having a mentor and network support has stronger career benefits. There are several potential reasons for this, and both mentors and mentees must be aware of these pitfalls to avoid them:

- *Seeking and providing career-enhancing mentor support.* There is some evidence that women use mentors for emotional support. This may be particularly the case where women work in male-dominated environments or where they have female mentors, which may help to debrief on broader topics such as sexism and childcare. It is, however, career-focused mentoring that will help women progress in their careers. Men are more likely to ask for and receive career-focused mentoring, which provides access to opportunities and sponsorship.[33]

- *Pay attention to mentoring quality, frequency of meetings and length of relationship.* Where mentors are mostly male, such as in senior echelons of an organization or in male-dominated environments, it is important to pay attention to the quality of a mentoring relationship between male mentor and female mentee. While women are just as capable as men of forming networks and mentoring relationships, women's relationships tend to be less beneficial. Where women are paired with male mentors, the lack of similarity in gender may decrease communication quality, the frequency of contact and the overall desire to keep the mentoring relationship going.[34] The affinity that is felt by a gender-matched mentoring relationship may encourage mentors to go further for their mentees than in a relationship where a mentor is paired with a mentee of the opposite sex.

- *Ensure that women have access to high-status mentors.* Furthermore, there is evidence that women have lower-status mentors than their male counterparts. And we know that the higher-status and the more senior the mentor, the more beneficial the career outcomes for the mentee. As a result, women may gain fewer benefits from mentoring.[35]

- *Ensure that mentors do not penalize female mentees for breaking gender norms.* In an exploratory study at the IBM Smarter Workforce Institute, my then colleague Dr Susie d'Mello and I explored the role of personality in getting access to mentoring. We found that in most cases both men and women were rewarded for behaving in line with gender expectations; however the quality of women's mentoring suffered more than that of their male colleagues when women's behaviour deviated from gender norms.[36] As would be expected, being calm and emotionally stable, as well as dependable and self-disciplined, increased mentoring quality for both men and women. Interestingly, while being disorganized, easily upset and uncreative decreased mentoring quality for both men and women, it did so much more significantly for women than for men. Furthermore, while both men and women were more likely to receive mentoring when they were seen to be sympathetic and warm, this was much more pronounced for women. Finally, while being disagreeable and quarrelsome significantly reduced women's likelihood of getting mentoring, it increased the chances of men getting mentoring. These findings require further exploration and replication but point to some potentially interesting gendered expectations that mentors may have of mentees and that mentors must be aware of to avoid them influencing the support they give their mentees.

## Reflection and encouragement

As we saw in Chapter 7, women, like men, benefit from reflecting on their experiences. Reflection encourages us to look inward and assess what went well and what did not go so well.

With reflection, however, we must ensure that women do not over-emphasize the areas they are less comfortable with at the expense of their strengths. It is also important to help women gain the confidence to apply for roles at a seniority level where there are few other women. With few other women around, a woman will become more visible and therefore more likely to be scrutinized. Some evidence emerged in the interviews that women may be holding themselves back from applying for more senior roles. This may not be surprising given the masculine definition of leadership. When a person is under increased scrutiny they are less likely to take risks and try new things. This is not unique to women; however, women tend to find themselves more often in this situation at senior levels in organizations.[37] Feedback can also be a double-edged sword for women. While their performance is often recognized by people around them, it is not that unusual for a woman to get gender-biased and confusing feedback such as 'be more decisive' and at the same time 'be less aggressive'. Women may particularly benefit from having the support of a coach to help them decode feedback and to reflect on their own strengths and development needs while still finding the courage to put themselves forward to a more senior role, even if they may not have all the skills and even if they are likely to be subjected to more scrutiny than their male counterparts. Other sources of support can be women-only development courses or a women's network that allows a safe area to debrief on these experiences and to retain a sense of purpose.[38]

## In practice: supporting women's career progression

Women only tend to apply for a role when they meet all the criteria. While it is important to have the skills that are required for the role, women must recognize that it is also about their potential to learn on the job. In this context, empowerment is important for women and having female role models is helpful to challenge the behavioural expectations we have of women. To effectively challenge our expectations of women, we must also challenge our expectations of men.

Felizitas Lichtenberg, Global Diversity &
Inclusion Manager, Vodafone

Women are often told they need more horizontal experience to step up to the next level. But they are not always given guidance about what experience to look for and they need to find this information themselves. Some either just work hard and wait, while others look for the experience externally. Those who look for broader experience internally are not always comfortable to ask for opportunities. Sometimes, they even ask for permission to speak to someone more senior about available roles. Some of the women feel that they don't have the experience to get the experience and say, 'What do I have to offer?' They often feel that they need certain things in place before they can ask for the experience. It's a vicious circle. I have observed similar things in other companies that I have worked for. It is not purely related to gender but also age. Senior women are more likely to say, 'I am going for this new job and although I don't have any technical experience, I bring logic and problem-solving – that's enough'. With experience comes confidence.

Rachel Osikoya, Head of Diversity & Inclusion, Global Transportation
and Logistics Organization

## The enabling role of HR

HR has several important roles to play. As we have already seen, when mentoring programmes are put in place, these need to be carefully designed and supported through training for both mentors and mentees. Furthermore, when designing high-potential programmes, it is important to consider how to design the (self-) nomination process, the selection process, the programme itself, as well as follow-on activities after the end of the programme. It is important to ensure that:

- women have the same opportunity to self-nominate or be nominated by their managers as their male counterparts;
- the programme structure enables women to access the same opportunities;
- the programme leads to women's progression and not a return to the same level or even the same role as before.

After working with organizations on the topic of women's career progression for many years, I have seen many instances where women are less frequently nominated to high-potential courses or where they simply return to the same role they held before the programme, while men are being promoted to significantly more challenging and senior roles.

Overcoming the 'think manager – think male' bias that we have talked about repeatedly in this chapter should not be exclusively HR's responsibility. However, HR can provide several solutions to reduce the likelihood of bias entering selection decisions.[39, 40, 41] These include, among others:

- Running unconscious bias training to raise awareness. The training is unlikely to eliminate bias. Bias is deep seated and will persist beyond the training session. Awareness raising events are nevertheless important to gain buy-in to more fundamental changes to HR processes.
- Using multiple sources of objective, high-quality psychometric measures to assess potential rather than relying solely on managers' assessment of potential.
- Using 'chunking' when evaluating interview responses, which means that every candidate's answers to a specific question are

rated anonymously in one batch. This means that the effects of an interview starting off well or less well, which tends to colour the rest of the interview, is removed.

- Hiring all senior roles in one batch rather than in separate recruitment events throughout the year. This makes it much more obvious if every recruit looks like each other.

## Summary

Women's reduced career progression can be seen clearly in the steadily decreasing numbers of women at higher organizational levels. Progress in getting more women to senior roles has been frustratingly slow. Women face two main barriers to their career progression: the 'think manager – think male' bias that aligns men's supposed characteristics of action-orientation and assertiveness with leadership qualities but not women's supposed characteristics of nurturing and caring. Furthermore, the continued expectation of women to act as the main caregivers means that they still carry most of the caring burden, which can often lead to reduced hours at work.

Those women who get to the top of an organization seem to get there on the fast track. Women on boards have been shown to be younger than their male counterparts, for example. Research into women's career progression has highlighted that the factors that are linked to accelerated leadership development also benefit women's career progression more generally: access to a breadth of different stretch assignments; access to the right networks and support; and taking risks and trying new roles. It is, however, also the case that women report a lower occurrence of these factors than men.

While women's performance tends to be evaluated as equally effective as that of men, at least for roles up to middle management, women are generally seen to be less ready for promotion than men. Furthermore, their gender roles come into conflict with definitions of leadership, particularly for senior leadership positions. Also, men have been found to define leadership in more masculine terms than women, which poses an additional hurdle since most senior decision-makers are still men. Data has shown that women tend to have less access to career-enhancing experiences such as turnaround projects, operational experience or international assignments.

To increase women's opportunities of accelerated career progression, organizations must tackle barriers at all levels and check HR processes and promotion criteria for unintended bias. While unconscious bias training cannot eliminate bias on its own, it can help raise awareness and secure buy-in to process changes that reduce the impact of bias on hiring and promotion decisions.

Important career stakeholders such as mentors must understand the impact of potential, unintentional bias in the support they provide to women. Furthermore, women need access to an 'old girls network', where it exists, for additional support. If there are not yet enough senior women to provide this support, women need access to sponsorship from senior men. Finally, in male-dominated environments, women may need additional encouragement to put themselves forward for senior roles. This support is helpful as women often face increased scrutiny in senior roles due to their novelty at higher organizational echelons. As we saw at the start of the book, only 25 per cent of senior roles are held by women. Women may also be more closely watched in senior roles as they are not seen as ideal candidates for these positions which are still largely associated with masculine characteristics.

## Organizational design tips

- **Address unconscious bias.** Unconscious bias is a subtle yet powerful brake on women's career acceleration. While unconscious bias training will raise awareness, it will not be able to reduce bias by itself. Instead, address bias in selection and promotion decisions by using objective measures to assess potential or techniques such as chunking to evaluate interview responses more objectively.

- **Provide access to critical job assignments.** Review your process for assigning your high-potential women to career-enhancing, high-visibility roles. Ensure that selection criteria do not favour masculine characteristics and that you do not make decisions on behalf of a woman. Instead, offer women the role irrespective of whether they have just come back from maternity leave or whether they have a young family. If now is not the right time for the person to take up the role, keep an ongoing dialogue to reassess whether their situation has changed.

- **Provide opportunities for networking with senior stakeholders in work time.** Access to senior networks is vital for women. Ensure that you provide opportunities for networking in work hours rather than leaving it up to the individual to build networks out of hours. Office-hours networking events help women with childcare conflicts. They also reduce the likelihood of any potential gossip. After-work drinks between a senior male leader and a more junior female employee may not always be interpreted in the most favourable light. As a result, both parties may be reluctant to seek these networking opportunities.

- **Design mentoring programmes carefully.** Ensure that mentoring programmes aimed at supporting the acceleration of women's career progression are carefully designed, including mentor and mentee training, careful matching of mentors and mentees and monitoring of mentoring quality.

## Individual coaching tips

- **Keep your career stakeholders informed about your achievements.** While overt self-promotion can misfire for women, it is important that your career stakeholders know what you have achieved. Women face an additional credibility barrier that they need to overcome. Being able to show that you have already delivered some outstanding results will help you secure your next role. If you find it uncomfortable to openly share your achievements, ask your mentor or line manager to advocate on your behalf.

- **Let go of the notion of being an expert.** We all love being good at what we do. When we try our hand at a variety of different things, we may have a greater breadth of experience but less depth. Women's career progression is often held back as their experience base is too narrowly focused. Try different roles and move across functions to build an organization-wide outlook and network.

- **Build on your transferable skills.** Accept that you will never be ready for a more senior role or a significantly different role. Nobody ever is. There will always be gaps in knowledge. Be confident that you will be able to learn any missing skills once you are in the new role.

- **Find the most senior or influential mentor possible.** Senior people have social clout, access to networks and a clear understanding of an organization's politics and its unwritten rules. Try to get the most senior mentor possible. People with senior mentors do better than those with less high-status mentors. We also benefit from different perspectives. While you may prefer a female mentor due to greater affinity, also consider a male mentor.

# Notes

**1** UK Office for National Statistics, *Women in the Labour Market*, 2013 (most recent data available at time of writing)

**2** UK Office for National Statistics, *Women in the Labour Market*, 2013

**3** Catalyst, *Pyramid: Women in S&P 500 Companies* (19 September 2016)

**4** US Bureau of Labor Statistics, *Women in Management*, 2017, available from https://www.bls.gov/careeroutlook/2017/data-on-display/women-managers.htm

**5** Grant Thornton Insights (2017) *Women in Business 2017*, Grant Thornton International

**6** Grant Thornton Insights (2017) *Women in Business 2017*, Grant Thornton International

**7** Catalyst Knowledge Centre, available from http://www.catalyst.org/knowledge/women-ceos-sp-500 (data accessed January 2018)

**8** High Pay Centre and the Chartered Institute of Personnel and Development (2017) *Executive pay: Review of FTSE 100 executive pay packages*

**9** European Women on Boards (2016) *Gender Diversity on European Boards. Realizing Europe's potential, progress and challenges*, a European Women on Boards study carried out in partnership with ISS

**10** European Institute for Gender Equality (2013) *Reconciliation of work and family life as a condition of equal participation in the labour market*

**11** Parker, K and Wang, W (2013) *Modern Parenthood Roles of Moms and Dads Converge as They Balance Work and Family*, Pew Research Center, Washington

**12** Schein, VE, Mueller, M, Lituchy, T and Liu, J (1996) Think Manager – Think Male: A Global Phenomenon?, *Journal of Organizational Behavior*, **17** (1), pp 33–41

**13** Eagly, A H and Karau, SJ (2002) Role congruity theory of prejudice toward female leaders, *Psychological Review*, **109** (3), pp 573–98

**14** Hopkins, MM, O'Neil, DA, Passarelli, A and Bilimoria, D (2008) Women's leadership development: Strategic practices for women and organizations, *Consulting Psychology Journal: Practice and Research*, **60**, pp 348–65, available from http://psycnet.apa.org/journals/cpb/60/4/348/

**15** Koenig, AM, Eagly, AH, Mitchell, AA and Ristikari, T (2011) Are leader stereotypes masculine? A meta-analysis of three research paradigms, *Psychological Bulletin*, **137**, pp 616–42

**16** Roth, PL, Purvis, KL and Bobko, P (2010) A meta-analysis of gender group differences for measures of job performance in field studies, *Journal of Management*, **20**, pp 1–20, available from http://jom.sagepub.com/content/38/2/719.short

**17** Lemelle, CJ, Carson, MA and Smith, BK (2013) Gender differences in 360 ratings: An exploration across TWO industries, presented as part of SIOP 2013 Symposium 'Current Advancements in Research on Women Leaders: Triumphs and Roadblocks', Euston, 2013

**18** Sullivan, K and Green, A (2013) WoMANUFACTURING: Ratings of manager quality by gender and environment, presented as part of SIOP 2013 Symposium 'Current Advancements in Research on Women Leaders: Triumphs and Roadblocks', Euston, 2013

**19** Ruderman, MN, Ohlott, PJ and Kram, KE (1996) *Managerial Promotion: The dynamics for men and women*, Center for Creative Leadership, Greensboro, NC, available from http://72.15.242.230/leadership/pdf/publications/readers/reader170ccl.pdf

**20** EY Center for Board Matters (2015) Women on US boards: what are we seeing?

**21** Cappelli, P, Hamori, M and Bonet, R (2014) Who's got those top jobs? *Harvard Business Review*, March, available from https://hbr.org.2014/03/whos-got-those-top-jobs

**22** Wichert, I (2014) *The Whole Package: Women's career progression in the context of work, home and family*, IBM Smarter Workforce Institute

**23** Wichert, I (2014) *The Whole Package: Women's career progression in the context of work, home and family*, IBM Smarter Workforce Institute

**24** Wichert, I (2014) *The Whole Package: Women's career progression in the context of work, home and family*, IBM Smarter Workforce Institute

**25** Ruderman, MN, Ohlott, PJ and Kram, KE (1996) *Managerial Promotion: The dynamics for men and women*, Center for Creative Leadership, Greensboro, NC, available from http://72.15.242.230/leadership/pdf/publications/readers/reader170ccl.pdf

**26** Kumra, S and Vinnicombe, S (2010) Impressing for Success: A gendered analysis of a key social capital accumulation strategy, *Women and Men in Management: Issues for the 21st Century*, **17** (5), pp 521–46, available from https://doi.org/10.1111/j.1468-0432.2010.00521.x

**27** Wichert, I and D'Mello, S (2013) A 3-Level, 11-Factor Women Leaders' Career Progression framework, Presented at SIOP, 2013

**28** Wichert, I (2011) *Where Have All the Senior Women Gone? 9 critical job assignments for women leaders*, Palgrave Macmillan, Basingstoke

**29** Paustian-Underdahl, SC, Rogelberg, S, King, E, Ordonez, Z, Wichert, I and Rasch, R (2014) Understanding the queen bee effect in the workplace: A cross-cultural examination, *Academy of Management Proceedings*, doi: 10.5465/AMBPP.2014.8*ACAD MANAGE PROC* January 2014 (Meeting Abstract Supplement) 10286

**30** Joecks, J, Pull, K and Vetter, K (2012) *Gender Diversity in the Boardroom and Firm Performance: What exactly constitutes a 'critical mass'?* University of Tübingen, available at academia.edu

**31** Konrad, AM, Kramer, V and Erkut, S (2008) Critical mass: The impact of three or more women on corporate boards, *Organizational Dynamics*, 37, pp 145–64

**32** Torchia, M, Calabro, A and Huse, M (2011) *Women directors on corporate boards: From tokenism to critical mass, Journal of Business Ethics*, vol 102, pp 299–317

**33** Broadbridge, A (2010) Social capital, gender and careers: evidence from retail senior managers, *Equality, Diversity and Inclusion: An International Journal*, vol 29, pp 815–34

**34** Ragins and McFarlin, 1990 and Tsui and O'Reilly, 1989 and Byrne, 1971 as quoted in Kirchmeyer, C (1998) Determinants of managerial career success: Evidence and explanation of male/female differences, *Journal of Management,* vol 24(6), pp 673–92

**35** Carter, NM and Silva, C (2010) *Mentoring: Necessary but insufficient for advancement,* Catalyst Inc, New York

**36** D'Mello, S and Wichert, I (2013) *The Relationship between Personality and Mentoring: Does protégée gender matter?* Presented at SIOP, 2013

**37** Ibarra, H, Ely, R, and Kolb, D (2013) Women rising: The unseen barriers, *Harvard Business Review*, September 2013

**38** Ibarra, H, Ely, R, and Kolb, D (2013) Women rising: The unseen barriers, *Harvard Business Review*, September 2013

**39** Wichert, I (2016) Unconscious bias training won't increase diversity, LinkedIn Blog. https://www.linkedin.com/pulse/unconscious-bias-training-wont-increase-diversity-ines-wichert/

**40** Five minutes with... David Halpern, *The Psychologist*, May 2017

**41** Bohnet, I (2016) *What Works: Gender equality by design,* Harvard University Press

# Millennials 10

## On the fast track from the start

*Millennials and Generation Z are very clear about their desire to have a clear development path. They want more transparency and clear sight of their next move. Our belief is that everyone owns his/ her own career. There are different ways we are bridging this gap: by role modelling successful graduates who are now holding leadership positions and by facilitating a talent marketplace.*

CATALINA SCHVENINGER, GLOBAL HEAD OF RESOURCING &
EMPLOYER BRAND, VODAFONE

*I don't want to rest on my laurels. Speed is important. I don't like the stale feeling when you are doing the same thing again and again and you are not learning.*

KRISTIE DALOIA MANAGER, MASTERCARD

*At the developing end of the organization it is clear what people are looking for; they want tangible insights and want to understand what roles are open in the organization along with what career paths there are.*

PAUL NIXON, GLOBAL TALENT & INCLUSION RELATIONSHIP MANAGER
(EUROPE, AUSTRALIA & NEW ZEALAND), MERCER

## Millennials: tomorrow's leaders

This last chapter of the book takes us right back to the start. In Chapter 1 we explored how the desire of millennials to progress faster, along with digital disruption and the challenges of the VUCA world, are drivers of accelerated leadership development. Organizations are taking millennials' wish for faster progression seriously, as millennials are organizations' pool of future leaders. By 2020, 46 per cent of the global workforce will be millennials.[1] Some 15 per cent are already leaders, a number that will double by 2025.[2] About 50 per cent of millennials report that they want to become leaders.[3, 4]

Millennials are often described as digital natives, a generation that grew up with technology central to their life experience. With millennials shaping the workplace, they have received a lot of interest as a generation. Definitions vary somewhat, but they are generally defined as people born between 1981 and 2000. It is important to note that older millennials are already in their late 30s and the group we are talking about in this chapter are predominantly the younger group who are now in the early part of their careers: younger millennials in their mid- to late 20s. A number of the quotes in this chapter are, however, from 'older' millennials who are already in leadership roles.

Two characteristics that have arguably demanded most of the spotlight are millennials' tendency to be less loyal to organizations and being a generation of entitlement – wanting to have everything now rather than waiting for it. We must be cautious, however, with statements about generational differences as any of these differences may be down to age rather than generation. As a Boomer or Gen X employee, it is easy to forget what life was like in one's 20s. Professor Ilke Iceoglu and her colleagues, for example, showed that our motivations change as we get older. While achievement and personal growth seem to be important when we are younger, these motivations become less important as we get older and personal principles and autonomy become priorities instead.[5]

My former IBM colleagues Dr Jack Wiley and Dr Rena Rasch ran a large-scale US cohort study (of non-IBM employees) that allowed them to control for the effects of age and time. The results showed that there is little difference between the generations. When it comes to work and pay satisfaction and, interestingly, turnover intentions, the differences between generations are negligible. While they found generational differences for company and job satisfaction, job security, career development, advancement and recognition, these differences were all small and showed millennials to be more positive than previous generations.[6] Although this research shows that there are no significant differences in turnover intentions, millennials, along with other generations, still consider leaving their employers. Various studies indicate that 25 to 30 per cent intend to leave their employer in the next 12 months and 45 to 50 per cent of millennials in the next two years.[7, 8, 9] This makes retention a key issue, given the strategic importance of this talent pool to organizations.

# Career expectations

To encourage millennials to stay with an organization, we must get a clearer understanding of what they are expecting from their careers. Millennials have often been characterized as highly individualistic, comfortable embracing emerging technology, and wanting to work toward meaningful tasks. They seek career advancement and skill development but also desire work–life balance. They have a high need for achievement and want development support. They also value inclusive leadership with access to immediate feedback and open communication, and they expect to express their thoughts, and opinions.[10] The In Practice box below illustrates some of these expectations well.

---

### In practice: millennials' career expectations

Is acceleration really about obtaining top management privileges such as a company car and travelling first class? In my opinion, for millennials it's more about being able to exert influence which is usually easier in senior roles. Millennials are more motivated when they have jobs where they are being heard, seen and respected. They want variety in the things they do as well as in their career opportunities.

Torsten Schmeichel, former Global Head of People Development, Global Microelectronics Organization

How do I define career success? I use my parents as an excellent example. It took me a long time to work out what they have achieved. They were not bound by jobs, companies or industries. They did what they loved. But success also yields happiness. A career could mean anything. I want to have a diverse and interesting career. My idea of a career is constantly evolving. In the past, I wanted to be a doctor, lawyer and journalist. You can be all of it, if you are willing to invest in it.

Nicholas W Morgan, Client & Business Development Associate, International Wealth Management Firm

I ran a focus group with junior people across the world and what came to mind for people when they talked about careers was different in each region. In Asia, it was about internal mobility. In the US, it was about interests and skills, and in Europe it was about breadth of work.

Michael Schwarz, Talent Consultant, Mercer

A career in a traditional sense is not very important to me. By that I mean being an employee for a long time with one employer. A career that matters is about aligning your environment so that you can add value. The status of being a leader is not a driver. I want to be in positions that enable others to deliver their value. I want to be an inspiration and provide a roadmap for others.

Alexander Nelson-Williams, Senior Management, Multinational Professional Services Firm in the 'Big Four'

Let us take a closer look at three of these characteristics:

- leadership;
- acceleration of progression;
- career clarity.

## Leadership, impact and making a difference

Recognition is motivating. I enjoyed working with our CEO and getting sponsorship from our senior team for the work I was doing. They supported my project.

Sarah Sanderson, Head of Diversity & Inclusion Intelligence, Global Business Insight and Talent Management Consultancy

As we saw earlier in this chapter, about 50 per cent of millennials want to become leaders. Furthermore, 71 per cent of those who state that they will leave their employer in the next two years are unhappy with how their leadership skills are being developed. This is 17 per cent higher than for the group who want to stay beyond five years.[11] The most loyal millennials are most likely to agree that they want a leadership role *and* that they are actively encouraged to take a leadership role. The least loyal, on the other hand, state that they have been overlooked for leadership positions and that their leadership skills are not being fully developed.[12]

However, when it comes to considering the price of leadership, in the form of increased levels of stress and long working hours, research from INSEAD Business School shows that not all millennials are equally hungry for leadership. In a study of just over 16,000 millennials across the world, millennials in Africa (70 per cent), Central & Eastern Europe and North America (both 67 per cent) are more willing to put up with more stress and longer working hours than their contemporaries in the Middle East and Western Europe where only 45 per cent and 56 per cent of millennials respectively indicated that they are happy to pay the price for leadership.[13] These results are supported by Deloitte's 2015 Millennial Survey, which showed that while only 54 per cent of millennials in Western Europe and 57 per cent in Latin America wanted to become leaders, this increased to 70 per cent for Asia and 73 per cent for BRIC (Brazil, Russia, India and China) countries.[14] North America ranked in the middle with 65 per cent. Also, millennials' reasons for wanting to become leaders differ across the world.[15] The top three attractions for millennials in a managerial or leadership role are:

- high future earnings;
- the opportunity to influence the organization;
- working with strategic challenges.

## Providing early opportunities for leadership and impact

Clearly, millennials want to make a difference. They are looking for roles that allow them to take on responsibility, to be heard and to work with senior leaders. Organizations can help generate opportunities for impact and early exposure to leadership through several approaches.

**Educating senior leaders and training line managers**    First, it is crucial to educate senior leaders about the importance of interacting with early-career talent. Younger high-potential employees seek this inter-action and they want the opportunity to be heard and share their views. Senior leadership teams must be open to these interactions and be ready to be challenged by younger talent. Furthermore, organizations will benefit from investing in line-manager training to help supervisors understand the importance of participative decision-making, recogni-tion of achievements and access to stretching roles. In an interesting study, early-career professionals were less inclined to leave an organi-zation when they perceived their supervisors to be supportive. This perceived supervisor support increased a young professional's attach-ment to their supervisor (emotional attachment, respect and pride), which in turn led to a decrease in turnover intentions. Supervisors can boost perceptions of support by providing access to challenging roles, giving young professionals a sense of accomplishment and the oppor-tunity to use their skills.[16] Also, graduates have reported that they see their ideal supervisor as a coach and mentor, or even a friend. They want their line managers to respect them and to support them with career progression, to trust them to get things done and to commu-nicate proactively. Supervisors, on the other hand see their roles as setting clear targets and giving performance feedback.[17] Investing in managers learning how to effectively balance performance manage-ment with opportunities for personal growth is likely to pay off in the form of higher engagement levels and lower turnover intentions among younger high-potential employees.

**Shadowing and action learning**    Second, providing shadowing oppor-tunities for early-career talent helps younger high-potential employees to get a better understanding for just how complex senior roles are and how much experience is required to manage these roles effec-tively. As a result, it may help to temper emerging talents' desire for fast progression. Alternatively, organizations should consider provid-ing emerging talent with opportunities to work on business projects as part of action-learning sets, which will allow them to get an early taste for interacting with senior leaders. As we saw in Chapter 4, action-learning sets are a method that is often used for accelerated development at mid-career but it can be adapted for less experienced talent by allowing them to work on important yet more clearly defined projects where outcomes are presented back to senior leaders.

### Agile work structures for distributed decision-making

In a traditional organizational set-up, someone is either a leader or they are not. In agile organizations, on the other hand, people's roles change: one day they lead a project, then they are part of another person's project. People will change roles more frequently and we will have fewer leaders.

Torsten Schneider, Director Human Resources,
Luther Rechtsanwaltsgesellschaft

Finally, organizations may benefit from introducing agile, project-based working structures, such as wirearchies or holacracies in parts of the organizations that lend themselves to testing such distributed decision-making work structures. Wirearchies are defined as 'a dynamic two-way flow of power and authority, based on knowledge, trust, credibility and a focus on results, enabled by interconnected people and technology'.[18] Holacracies, on the other hand, are work structures that are defined by flexible project roles, which replace static job descriptions, where change is achieved through rapid iterations rather than one-off big re-organizations, where transparent rules displace office politics and importantly, where delegated authority becomes distributed authority.[19] These work structures provide early opportunities for taking on responsibility and having impact while at the same time providing an organization with increased agility.

## *Accelerated development*

My challenge is answering the question: 'Where do you want to be in five years' time?' If I decide I want it in five years, then what is stopping me from being able to achieve it now? Therefore, speed is very important for me.

Laura Tolen, Partnership Director,
International Logistics Organization

Millennials *want* accelerated leadership development. Fast career progression often emerges as a key engagement driver for this talent group. Over half of millennials state that they are afraid of getting stuck in a job with no opportunities to develop.[20] Organizations are working on putting in place solutions to enable accelerated development for millennials. This often happens with the background of millennials' career restlessness and the increased risk of losing a millennial to another organization. As we saw in Chapter 4, organizations choose early careers as one of the two acceleration points for their high-potential employees. However, accelerated development programmes are often only available for a small number of early-career employees. This puts the onus of development on the high-potential millennial, a topic we already encountered in Chapter 2 and one we will come back to shortly. Another important driver of acceleration is breadth of experience.

## Breadth early on

> Breadth is very important and getting it early means you won't get pigeon-holed as either a generalist or a specialist. Also, the cost of failure is lower.
>
> Stephen Caulfield, Vice President Global Field
> Services & GM Dell Bratislava, Dell EMC Global Services

To enable millennials to progress at pace and get to roles where they can have impact and influence, the HR and business leaders I interviewed talked about the need for breadth. As we already saw in Chapter 2, moving across functions is a key accelerator for careers. And as we saw in Chapter 4, providing breadth early on is a positive experience for millennial leaders and beneficial for the organization. Not only does it reduce the potential impact if anything goes wrong, as roles are at a more junior level, it also helps to provide emerging talent with the opportunity to build an organization-wide perspective. The start of a career is also the time when employees are more likely to want to move, before getting too focused on one area or one geography.

However, with millennials' focus on progressing upward, it is important to help them understand how side steps add value and provide the foundation for senior roles. We shouldn't take their understanding of the importance of breadth for granted. Younger talent still seems to have a focus on developing technical expertise, which is not surprising. After starting with little or no technical expertise when they first enter the workplace, learning to be good at something is a positive experience that increases their satisfaction levels and sense of mastery. During this 'getting established' phase younger professionals tend to focus mostly on validating their behaviours in a work context and building their skills and experience set.[21]

One of the core experiences that we encountered in Chapter 3, international experience, emerged as the lowest priority in a survey of over 1,000 millennials from five countries (UK, US, Brazil, China and Japan) when compared to 14 other factors that millennials consider important for their careers. Less than half the respondents from the US, UK and France regarded it as important. It ranked higher for millennials from Brazil, China and India. We must help emerging leaders to not get too focused on developing deep technical expertise and instead help them understand how breadth at the start of their careers can be the foundation for more challenging roles later.

## Helping millennials gain career breadth and speed

Organizations can help emerging leaders gain access to a range of different roles through several approaches, including the creation of a risk-embracing development culture, networking training and career guidance.

**Creating a risk-embracing development culture**   Millennials' impatience and desire for faster progression is a push factor for accelerated development. As a result, organizations are bringing down the target age for senior-level roles, in some cases as early as the early 30s. To allow emerging leaders to get ready for senior roles in a shorter period, organizations must be ready to take more risks and appoint younger talent to stretch roles. However, there is a general concern among senior leaders that high-potential talent may not be ready to move at an accelerated pace. This fear is particularly pronounced about millennials who are often still relatively inexperienced. To help overcome this fear, we must educate senior leaders that it no longer takes 25 years to get to the top; career decision-makers must embrace a faster speed of progression than in the past to avoid a continued collision course between millennials' drive for speed and an organization's risk aversion, a danger we already explored in detail in Chapter 6.

**Networking training**   A powerful support mechanism that organizations may benefit from providing for their millennials is networking training. Plenty of research has shown that career success is essentially a combination of hard work and receiving sponsorship from more senior members of the organization.[22] Learning how to network allows a young high-potential employee to access information, identify job opportunities, increase their visibility, ask for help and find experts to help with unfamiliar tasks in a new stretch assignment. Networking training may be particularly important for those early-career professionals who are not forced to build new relationships as part of their job. Training can help to demystify networking and can help millennials develop elevator pitches and practise through speed-dating games. They will also benefit from an assessment of their networking activities and receiving feedback on what else they can do to build a network of relevant contacts.[23]

## Career guidance and internal job market

> We have career stories that are popular as they show progression and stepping stones. Lots of people have filled one out. They are one-page visuals of a person's career and include personal milestones, such as taking time out for family. People like seeing unconventional career paths.
> Paul Nixon, Global Talent & Inclusion Relationship
> Manager (Europe, Australia & New Zealand), Mercer

Furthermore, organizations can prevent millennials from getting lost in the organization by providing career frameworks and career profiles of successful executives. While it may be difficult for an organization to set out a precise career path, millennials will nevertheless benefit from understanding the various directions in which their careers could develop. In large and complex organizations it may also pay off to proactively share job opportunities and career information from different parts of the organization. Several HR leaders I talked to recounted experiences where high-potential employees who wanted to get a different role left the organization rather than talk to their manager about getting access to this type of role at the current organization. One solution is to make sure that all available roles in an organization are advertised. This also helps to increase diversity with job applications as jobs are not 'handed out' within a senior leader's own network. As a result, a much wider range of candidates is encouraged to apply for the role. Internal marketplaces will give a millennial a better understanding of what types of roles are available in the organization and enable them to find challenging roles. The onus is still on the emerging leader to identify and secure the roles; however, the organization puts in place the necessary infrastructure to enable this more easily.

**Onboarding**   Finally, speed of progression can be increased through effective onboarding of a millennial employee into their new role. While onboarding is often only provided for new starters in an organization, actively helping a person get to grips with their new role and getting them to peak performance faster will increase career velocity. Organizations may benefit from working with the millennial's new line manager or a sponsor to specify the following four areas of information for a millennial as part of their onboarding process:

- knowing why – the purpose of the new role;
- knowing what – the key deliverables of the role;
- knowing how – identifying critical skills and knowledge that must be mastered and acquired quickly;
- knowing who – important stakeholders.

Furthermore, regular feedback about the employee's performance will allow the emerging leader to adjust their behaviour and become effective more quickly.

---

### In practice: accelerating millennials' careers

Millennials think about careers all the time. I am a boomer and when I was in my 20s, I was told that it would take time to progress. That is gone now. They are ready to move, are good at navigating careers and think that anything is possible. We spend a lot of time hiring for potential and then we train them further on the graduate programme. Then we lose sight of them before they pop up to become a manager. People used to get lost in the past. We now want to make a difference and find the best way to give them an understanding of what it would be like to be a leader.
Michael Heil, Global Head of Talent Management, The Linde Group

To fully graduate as an engineer takes a minimum of four years. You cannot accelerate this. The engineers are driven by mastery. The restlessness then sets in at Year 5. Other talent gets restless earlier. They always want to know what project is next. They want stretch and to be deployed on challenging projects. They want technical progression and peer recognition. We help them to be aware of the range of choices and who to build relationships with. We also help them be conscious of what support they are getting. We do a lot on internal network building. It is our marketplace. People want to build experiences to share at these networks. We try to harness the concept of the gig economy. You choose your gigs with support from your manager.

> Jennifer Duvalier, Non-Executive Director, Mitie plc,
> Guardian Media Group plc, Royal College of Arts

How does a company take the best of these young people for three to four years? They tend to rotate from company to company. It is about hiring the right profile and enabling speedy, accelerated integration. They need to be doing their role well quickly. Don't complicate things, give them the freedom to work at their best. Allow them to propose things, be proactive, have a different schedule and to express themselves. Measure by results. Provide them with cross-functional projects, get them exploring new ways of approaching new markets and doing R&D. We must use these new ideas and integrate them with those of different generations.

> Susana Simões, Regional Lead EMEA, Learning &
> Development, Global Electronics Organization

If I think about what opportunities were available to me when I was younger versus those available to people now. Today, people are much more collaborative. They want flexibility and opportunity. They think about careers in three-year chunks. I would be delighted if I got five years from people. We have a development strategy to help people stay for longer, but it is based on mutual benefit. We offer colleagues the opportunity to study for a master's degree, a really innovative programme that the company fully funds. In return we ask them to commit to the organization for longer. As a result, people are contributing more and staying for longer. It works for everybody.

> Andy Doyle, former CHRO, Worldpay Group plc

## *Career clarity: what's next?*

In addition to wanting responsibility earlier on and having the opportunity to work on meaningful projects, millennials want clarity about their next career move. This is an observation most of the HR leaders whom I talked to shared: 'Millennials always want to know what is next'. This means that millennials want to see a clear path for their career and a good understanding of open roles. There is a desire to understand the next step. The focus is more in the here and now rather than too far into the future. They also want to get feedback about their own performance and want to understand how well they are doing. This desire for clear career steps and a structured career path also emerged unanimously from the millennials I interviewed for this book and those whom I have worked with and mentored. Clarity of career steps is critical to them.

### Career self-management

This desire for clarity puts millennials on a potential collision course with how organizations think about career management. We have already talked about organizations' reliance on high-potential employees' initiative and career self-management. As part of this, organizations expect millennials to explore their next job move rather than have the organization map this out for them. Many organizations are moving away from defining clear career paths as these can quickly become outdated in the wake of organizational restructures. Furthermore, many organizations are very short-term focused, which means that it is often not possible to let someone know where they will be in 12 or 18 months' time.

Career self-management is a three-stage process:[24]

1 Career exploration. A millennial gathers information about their own strengths, development needs, values and interests.

2 Career goals. The emerging leader sets out the goals they want to achieve.

3 Career strategies. The high-potential employee engages in a set of activities to help achieve their career goals. Examples of such activities are:

**a**  networking;

**b**  increasing visibility;

**c**  positioning behaviour;

**d**  increasing skills through training and development;

**e**  managing work–life balance.

## Career management courses versus career communities

While it may be tempting to offer millennials courses on career self-management as an enabler, it is important to ensure that these are not one-off events where the message of the course stands in stark contrast to the organizational realities. There is evidence that where career management courses are offered as a mandatory, one-off HR initiative, these may lead to a decrease rather than an increase in career management. The reasons for this may be that participants are reacting negatively to the mandatory nature of an event that puts the onus of action on them, or they are frustrated by the mismatch between a message about the organization expecting career self-management and the reality where information, infrastructure and opportunities for successful self-management are not available.[25] Another challenge is that many organizations rely on managers to help emerging talent chart their careers. Millennials' desire for information is often not met by their managers, either because the manager is not focused enough on their team's development or they lack the skill and training to have effective career conversations.

This study emphasizes the danger of advocating career self-management without effectively enabling it. Career self-management must not become a misnomer for no career management. Instead of attending career management courses, millennials may benefit from career management communities where they can meet like-minded peers, exchange information, learn to network and build organization-wide contacts.

## Creating virtuous cycles

There is also evidence that if organizations rely too much on career self-management and provide little or no formal career development support, this may increase a millennial's likelihood of leaving the organization.[26] As a result, organizations must develop virtuous cycles whereby millennials' career self-management and initiative is met with enhanced access to organizational support, such as mentors, training and development and career opportunities.[27] To achieve this, HR must provide the necessary 'scaffolding' for millennial talent as well as direct support through managers and mentors, all three of which we have already discussed in Chapter 8. As we have seen in this chapter, and as summarized in Figure 10.1, organizations can take a number of steps to help millennials achieve early exposure to leadership, to accelerate their learning and their careers, and to create greater career clarity.

**Figure 10.1**  Organizational enablers of millennials' careers

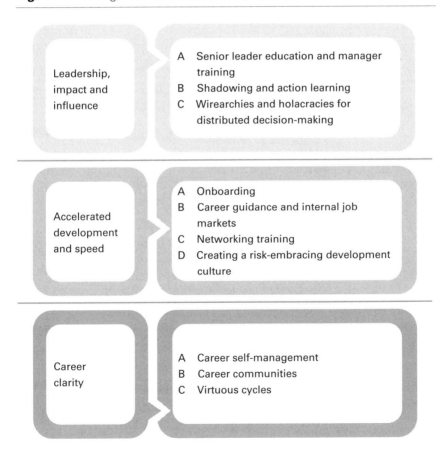

Leadership, impact and influence
- A  Senior leader education and manager training
- B  Shadowing and action learning
- C  Wirearchies and holacracies for distributed decision-making

Accelerated development and speed
- A  Onboarding
- B  Career guidance and internal job markets
- C  Networking training
- D  Creating a risk-embracing development culture

Career clarity
- A  Career self-management
- B  Career communities
- C  Virtuous cycles

# Summary

Millennials have received a lot of attention due to their apparent differences in work attitudes when compared to other generations. While data shows that millennials are not all that different, they are nevertheless motivated by fast career progression, a readiness to leave their current employer and a desire to have influence and impact. Data also shows that millennials are not a homogeneous group and vary across the globe in their career expectations and fears.

Millennials' desire for accelerated leadership development is motivated by a desire to move to roles where they can have impact and influence. Furthermore, it is driven by a desire to keep growing and developing and a dislike of being bored. Given the strategic importance of millennials as a talent group, organizations are paying attention to millennials' desire to progress fast. As a minimum, many organizations are providing support and infrastructures that allow younger high-potential employees to effectively self-manage their career. This includes support such as clear guidance, networking training and internal marketplaces. Organizations must also help millennials understand the importance of acquiring breadth of experience as a foundation for acceleration. The most promising and motivated millennials are then chosen for more formal development programmes.

Alongside speed, career clarity is a key consideration for millennials. Younger high-potential employees want to understand where their next role is going to be. This puts them on a potential collision course with their employer as many organizations no longer provide career paths for fear of seeing them outdated quickly after organizational reorganizations. Furthermore, many organizations are short-term focused and are often not able to let a high-potential millennial know where their next role in 12 or 18 months' time will be.

Also, organizations must overcome a friction between millennials on the one hand, who feel that they are able to take on significant roles despite limited experience, and risk-averse leaders on the other who value experience over potential. This is an area where HR plays an important role in helping to bring both parties closer together by educating senior leaders about the need for accelerated development, while providing mentors and shadowing opportunities for high-potential millennials to understand the extent and complexity of senior roles.

## Organizational design tips

- **Use data to develop your global millennial development strategy.** Millennials are not a homogeneous group. If you are responsible for a global cohort of early-career professionals, ensure that you understand the differences in career drivers across countries. Gather objective data and compare it to data from respondents in other generations. Millennials may be more like older generations in their own countries, but more diverse as a group between countries than is often portrayed in the popular media.

- **Create a virtuous cycle.** If your organization expects its employees to manage their own careers, create a virtuous cycle by supporting those high-potential employees who have demonstrated motivation and initiative with access to more formal career support, such as mentoring and training. Without this in place, your most promising millennials are at increased risk of leaving the organization for a lack of career development.

- **Provide as much career clarity as possible.** You may not be able to tell a young high-potential employee exactly what role they will get next but provide as much clarity as possible. This may be information about promotion criteria, career management resources that the emerging leader can tap into, or people they can talk to. Where career paths do not exist, help them understand how other people have charted their careers and what experience the organization values.

- **Provide career self-management infrastructure.** Review your career management offering and check whether it is a basic provision or active management of careers, whether it is a one-way or two-way exchange of career information between the emerging leader and the organization. Identify any gaps in your provision and add missing resources. If you are in the process of reviewing your career management offering, consult your young high-potential employees on the resources they want. Ensure that your statements about the importance of career self-management are supported by adequate infrastructure to allow the emerging leader to effectively manage their own career.

- **Provide access to senior leaders**. Ensure that senior leaders play an active role in the development of emerging leaders by acting as mentors or sponsors. Provide regular networking opportunities for senior leaders and younger talent in the organization. Ask senior leaders to talk about their own career journeys.

- **Help millennials understand the importance of breadth**. Career pathing information should not only focus on showing career paths upwards but also emphasize the importance of sideway moves as a foundation for the move to the top. Use early rotation programmes, career spiderwebs, a clear definition of the most important experiences to be gained and personal career stories that highlight diverse backgrounds to help young talent develop a holistic view of careers early on.

## Individual coaching tips

- **Turn your own career management into a development project**. Actively manage your own career. Treat it as a project where you can show early leadership qualities such as initiative taking, accountability, resourcefulness and networking. Furthermore, use your career management project to demonstrate that you are good at spotting opportunities and are ready to take risks to capitalize on these. Learn the fine art of sharing your successes and achievements without bragging. Gaining visibility for your efforts will increase your chances of securing access to more formal development opportunities.

- **Be prepared to push through difficult times**. Be ready to push through difficult times in a role and show determination to deliver outcomes even if this does not generate as much recognition as you would like or if success is not guaranteed. A vital leadership characteristic, no matter whether you are an individual contributor or whether you are leading the entire organization, is grit and perseverance. Without having demonstrated that you are willing to work at things, you may at some point no longer be considered for important or interesting projects.

- **Shadow senior people and gain an insight into their roles**. Take time to understand the nuances of senior roles, with all their complexity and ambiguity. Also look for early opportunities to lead a project, either at work or outside of work to gain experience of the challenges linked to leadership, such as motivating people to deliver outstanding results, making difficult decisions without having all the necessary information available and getting a diverse group of stakeholders to collaborate. This will allow you to understand what skills you have to develop and to demonstrate that you are aware of your strengths and development needs, an important leadership quality.

# Notes

**1** Loew, L (2015) *State of Leadership Development 2015: The time to act is now*, Brandan Hall Group

**2** Loew, L (2015) *State of Leadership Development 2015: The time to act is now*, Brandan Hall Group

**3** Loew, L (2015) *State of Leadership Development 2015: The time to act is now*, Brandan Hall Group

**4** *The 2016 Deloitte Millennial Survey: Winning over the next generation of leaders*

**5** Iceoglu, I, Segers, J and Bartram, D (2011) Age-related differences in work motivation, *Journal of Occupational and Organizational Psychology*, **85**, pp 300–29

**6** Kowske, BJ, Rasch, R and Wiley, J (2010) Millennials' (lack of) attitude problem: An empirical examination of generational effects on work attitudes, *Journal of Business and Psychology*, **25**, pp 265–79

**7** *The 2016 Deloitte Millennial Survey: Winning over the next generation of leaders*

**8** Ashridge Business School (2014) *The Millennial Compass: Truth about the 30-and-under millennial generation in the workplace*, with MSL Group

**9** Kowske, BJ, Rasch, R and Wiley, J (2010) Millennials' (lack of) attitude problem: An empirical examination of generational effects on work attitudes, *Journal of Business and Psychology*, **25**, pp 265–79

**10** Shih Yung Chou (2012) Millennials in the workplace: A conceptual analysis of millennial's leadership and followership styles, *International Journal of Human Resource Studies*, **2**, pp 71–83

**11** *The 2016 Deloitte Millennial Survey: Winning over the next generation of leaders*

**12** *The 2016 Deloitte Millennial Survey: Winning over the next generation of leaders*

**13** Universum Global (2014) *Understanding a misunderstood generation*, in partnership with INSEAD Business School, Emerging Markets Institute and The Head Foundation

**14** *The 2015 Deloitte Millennial Survey: Mind the gaps*

**15** Universum Global (2014) *Understanding a misunderstood generation*, in partnership with INSEAD Business School, Emerging Markets Institute and The Head Foundation

**16** Stinglhamber, F and Vandenberghe, C (2003) Organizations and supervisors as sources of support and targets of commitment: A longitudinal study, *Journal of Organizational Behavior*, **24**, pp 251–70

**17** *Great Expectations: Managing Generation Y* (2017) Institute of Leadership & Management and Ashridge Business School

**18** www.wirearchy.com

**19** www.holacracy.org

**20** Universum Global (2014) *Understanding a misunderstood generation*, in partnership with INSEAD Business School, Emerging Markets Institute and The Head Foundation

**21** Sturges, J (2008) All in a day's work? Career self-management and the management of the boundary between work and non-work, *Human Resource Management Journal*, **18**, pp 118–34

**22** Ng, TWH, Eby, LT, Sorensen, KL and Feldman, DC (2005) Predictors of objective and subjective career success: a meta-analysis, *Personnel Psychology*, **58**, pp 367–408

**23** De Janasz, SC and Forret, ML (2008) Learning the art of networking: A critical skill for enhancing social capital and career success, *Journal of Management Education*, **32**, pp 629–50

**24** Noe, R (1996) Is career management related to employee development and performance? *Journal of Organizational Behavior*, **17**, pp 119–33

**25** Kossek, EE, Roberts, K, Fisher, S and Demarr, B (1998) Career self-management: A quasi-experimental assessment of the effects of a training intervention, *Personnel Psychology*, **51**, pp 935–60

**26** Sturges, J, Guest, D, Conway, N and Mackenzie Davey, K (2002) A longitudinal study of the relationship between career management and organizational commitment among graduates in the first ten years of work, *Journal of Organizational Behavior*, **23**, pp 731–48

**27** Sturges, J, Guest, D, Conway, N and Mackenzie Davey, K (2002) A longitudinal study of the relationship between career management and organizational commitment among graduates in the first ten years of work, *Journal of Organizational Behavior*, **23**, pp 731–48

# INDEX

Note: Page numbers in *italics* indicate Figures or Tables.